Migrating from Xamarin.Forms to .NET MAUI

A Comprehensive Guide

Iris Classon

Apress®

Migrating from Xamarin.Forms to .NET MAUI: A Comprehensive Guide

Iris Classon
Mölndal, Sweden

ISBN-13 (pbk): 979-8-8688-1214-9   ISBN-13 (electronic): 979-8-8688-1215-6
https://doi.org/10.1007/979-8-8688-1215-6

Copyright © 2025 by Iris Classon

Managing Director, Apress Media LLC: Welmoed Spahr
Acquisitions Editor: Ryan Byrnes
Development Editor: Laura Berendson
Editorial Assistant: Gryffin Winkler

Cover designed by eStudioCalamar

Cover image by Bettina Nørgaard from Pixabay

Distributed to the book trade worldwide by Springer Science+Business Media New York, 1 New York Plaza, Suite 4600, New York, NY 10004-1562, USA. Phone 1-800-SPRINGER, fax (201) 348-4505, e-mail orders-ny@springer-sbm.com, or visit www.springeronline.com. Apress Media, LLC is a California LLC and the sole member (owner) is Springer Science + Business Media Finance Inc (SSBM Finance Inc). SSBM Finance Inc is a **Delaware** corporation.

For information on translations, please e-mail booktranslations@springernature.com; for reprint, paperback, or audio rights, please e-mail bookpermissions@springernature.com.

Apress titles may be purchased in bulk for academic, corporate, or promotional use. eBook versions and licenses are also available for most titles. For more information, reference our Print and eBook Bulk Sales web page at http://www.apress.com/bulk-sales.

Any source code or other supplementary material referenced by the author in this book is available to readers on GitHub. For more detailed information, please visit https://www.apress.com/gp/services/source-code.

If disposing of this product, please recycle the paper

To my phenomenal team at Plejd, your hard work, ingenuity, and dedication have been truly inspiring, and I am incredibly grateful for everything I've learned from you.

To the programming community, a welcoming and inspiring group whose collective knowledge and fervent dedication make this profession feel like home.

A special thanks to my wonderful husband Emanuel, who, with love and patience, managed our two lively boys, giving me the time and space to immerse myself in writing.

Table of Contents

About the Author

 **Iris Classon** isn't new to the XAML tech scene. Having navigated the waters of Silverlight, Windows Phone, Windows Store, Xamarin, and now MAUI, her expertise is broad and deep. Currently, she's in the trenches, part of a team steering a large-scale, complex application over a million users, from Xamarin.Forms to MAUI. This not only fuels her insights in this book but also ensures that the guidance comes from someone who's well-versed in making the leap from theory to action in the world of app migration.

Iris has held the title of Microsoft MVP for 12 years and has authored half a dozen technical books on .NET. Additionally, she has produced a wide array of Pluralsight and YouTube tutorials, along with Microsoft Learn tutorials and numerous hands-on workshops catering to a range from beginners to advanced users. She frequently speaks at conferences and user groups and keeps an active blog. Her entire professional life is dedicated to teaching, learning, and disseminating information about .NET, her platform of choice. Writing is a particular passion of hers; having published 13 books, some of which have been translated into several languages, it's clear that writing is not only her preferred way to share knowledge but also something she deeply enjoys.

About the Technical Reviewer

 **Denis Kondratev** has devoted more than 19 years to software development in various fields. For more than ten years, he was deeply involved in the field of security systems, where he applied and developed his skills in C++ and .NET. Currently, he is engaged in developing computer games using artificial intelligence technologies. He had the opportunity to work on games such as *Homescapes*, *Left To Survive*, and others, which have earned hundreds of millions of dollars. His articles have been published on popular technical platforms, such as hackernoon.com and dzone.com. He also regularly speaks at professional conferences, sharing his experience and knowledge with colleagues. You can learn more about him on LinkedIn (`https://www.linkedin.com/in/kondratev-denis`).

Acknowledgments

This book would not have come to life without the support and expertise of many talented individuals.

First, my sincere thanks to my editors, Deepa Tryphosa and Shonmirin P. A., for their invaluable insights and careful attention to detail. Your guidance has been instrumental in shaping this work.

To Denis Kondratev, our technical reviewer, thank you for your thorough and expert approach in ensuring the accuracy of the content.

A special thanks to Ryan Byrnes, acquisitions editor, for championing this project from the start.

I am incredibly grateful to my colleagues Johannes, Pontus, and Roger, whose hard work and dedication carried much of the heavy lifting in our migration efforts. To the rest of the team at Plejd—Max, Andreas, Marcus, Stefan, Daniel, Jimmy, Joel, Herman, David, Victor, and Magnus—thank you for your commitment, teamwork, and willingness to tackle every challenge. Working alongside such talented and supportive individuals is a privilege.

This book is a reflection of all that I've learned with you, and I am grateful to be part of such an exceptional team.

Introduction

Over a decade ago, when I first started learning programming, I created my very first app, which was a Windows Phone app. The curriculum at school primarily revolved around web development using Microsoft technologies; however, my participation in a Windows Phone user group sparked my passion for Windows Phone. This was my first introduction to XAML and marked the beginning of a journey that I am still actively pursuing. I made a hilarious blunder when I forgot to change the app name in the configuration file when I ported the app to iOS, and as a result, the installed app ended up being named *App1*. It took me a week to realize this after the app was launched, and embarrassment briefly replaced my sense of accomplishment. Swearing never to repeat that mistake or make new mistakes, I later realized that I had forgotten to include a divide by zero check in the algorithm. It's safe to say that I've learned many lessons throughout the years, and I've made it my personal mission to help others as much as possible by sharing what I've learned.

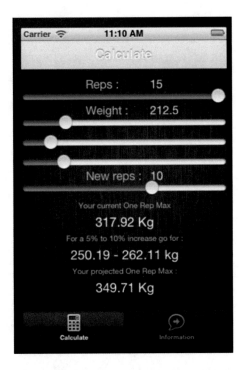

My first app was a Windows Phone app that was later ported to iOS.

Since App1, I've made many applications for Windows Phone and later Windows Store. I won a hackathon with Shake a Kitty, was featured on BBC World News with my marathon app, made a training course, and wrote a book about Windows Store app development. Prior to Xamarin's acquisition by Microsoft, I had the opportunity to visit the Xamarin head office and even got to engage in interesting discussions with Miguel De Icaza, the former cofounder of Xamarin. On a lighter note, I may have gone a bit overboard by accumulating more Tamarin Monkeys than any sensible adult should possess, as they were the beloved mascots of Xamarin. I still have one or two somewhere in the attic, and I'm sure my sons will be thrilled if I find the monkeys.

It's safe to say that I was, and still am, a big fan of cross-platform development with XAML and C#.

Today, I work as an app developer at Plejd, a supplier of smart lighting solutions. The success of the company heavily relies on the Plejd app, and during the migration from Xamarin.Forms to .NET MAUI, we had to be incredibly thorough despite the added challenge of launching new products at the same time. This book extensively draws on our migration experience, coupled with the knowledge I've accumulated over the years. Reflecting my development history, I will use a fictional yet functional application to demonstrate the migration steps and share valuable insights. It's a fitness application, and it's called *AppForFitness*.

Purpose of the Book

The primary goal of this book is to guide you through the process of migrating an application from Xamarin.Forms to .NET MAUI. By using a working application, I will demonstrate the migration process in a hands-on and structured manner. The chapters of the book are carefully crafted to build upon each other, introducing practical tips, fundamental ideas, and in-depth explorations whenever necessary.

The secondary goal is to address common questions, cover best practices, discuss alternatives, and address how you can stay up to date.

This book is primarily for Xamarin.Forms developers looking to migrate to .NET MAUI, as well as .NET developers interested in cross-platform development.

Whether you're a seasoned developer or new to cross-platform development, this guide will equip you with the knowledge and tools needed to make a successful transition to .NET MAUI.

Importance of Migration

The end of support (EOS) for Xamarin.Forms marks a significant milestone for those of us who have relied on this framework for cross-platform mobile development. The announcement was particularly alarming for several reasons. It meant no more official updates, including crucial security patches and bug fixes. And while this is absolutely concerning for developers, it didn't add as much urgency as the next reason. The foremost reason developers were alarmed was that there wouldn't be support for the latest versions of Xcode, and new versions of Xcode are often required to build and submit applications to the Apple App Store. This meant that without support for the latest Xcode version, developers risked being unable to release updates or new applications altogether.

I'll never forget how stressed my team was when the announcement was made. We were 15 people on the team, and 10 of us dove headfirst into migrating the app pressured by time while the rest worked on new products. The app is crucial for Plejd, and without the app we could literally leave customers in the dark if we failed to migrate in time. It took a month just to get to the point where we could build the app and another month to navigate between a couple of views. We ran into problem after problem, and the documentation and forums at the time were of little help. Just as we ran into the biggest wall yet, Microsoft announced they would release one final version with support for the next version of Xcode, which would buy developers a little bit more time. This also meant that Microsoft had more time to work on .NET MAUI, enrich the documentation, provide migration tools, and, most importantly, fix a lot of bugs. With the additional time, my team could convene and carefully outline the migration plan, distribute resources effectively, and ensure that our internal and external release targets were in sync. But the pressure was still there, as there definitely wouldn't be more Xamarin.Forms releases. There was only one path forward for us, and that was MAUI.

Once we got over the biggest hurdle, which was getting the app to build, we quickly discovered the upside of migrating to .NET MAUI. The app would build and deploy to the simulator in seconds, and the app was faster on both Android and iOS. We could remove several of our custom renderers and use built-in methods and properties instead, the layout controls were more flexible, resource management was easier, and so much more. But, as mentioned, we also ran into challenges. We couldn't get a multi-project structure to work, and the single project structure took a while to get used to. We had to rewrite our base layouts, the compatibility libraries caused more issues than they solved, navigation had to be redone, and so on. But all in all, we came out on the other side with a better and faster app and, most importantly, a future-proof app.

Structure and Approach

The book begins with an overview over .NET MAUI and the evolution from Xamarin.Forms. We then cover .NET MAUI features, alternatives, and common questions. And after establishing this foundation, we begin the migration process and follow through one step at a time.

Each step begins with a section that provides the necessary background information that explains the importance of the step and its relevance in the context of migration. After laying the groundwork, the chapter explains what the step comprises. This includes detailed descriptions of the tasks involved, the objectives we want to achieve, and the expected outcomes. At the core of each chapter is a hands-on example with the AppForFitness that shows the steps in action. This practical approach allows you to see the concepts being applied in real-world scenarios. The examples are carefully chosen to cover common use cases and potential challenges you might encounter during the migration.

Each chapter concludes with a summary that recaps the key points covered and provides a quick reference for reviewing the material later.

To ensure your migration is successful, the final chapters provide a range of additional resources and a troubleshooting guide.

Summary

Over a decade ago, my programming journey began with a Windows Phone app, sparking a lasting passion for mobile development and XAML. It's with this passion that I've written this book that guides you through a migration process using a hands-on, structured approach with a fictional fitness app, AppForFitness. Each chapter provides background information, foundational concepts, and practical examples, addressing common questions, best practices, and alternatives. The end of support for Xamarin.Forms underscores the urgency of this transition, ensuring apps remain functional and future-proof with .NET MAUI.

CHAPTER 1

The Evolution from Xamarin.Forms

To better understand the transition from Xamarin.Forms to .NET MAUI, it's essential to know a little about the origins and development of the platform. In this chapter, I will summarize the history of Xamarin and Xamarin.Forms, from inception to development, acquisition, and transition to .NET MAUI. With this foundation established, I will then address common questions about migration.

Xamarin to MAUI: A Brief History

Xamarin's story starts all the way back in 1999, with Miguel de Icaza and Nat Friedman. The two of them cofounded Helix Code, later known as Ximian. The company focused on GNOME-oriented software and Mono, a project that aimed to implement Microsoft's .NET development platform. When Ximian was acquired in 2011, Miguel de Icaza started Xamarin (Figure 1-1), a company that developed a platform for mobile app development. In the subsequent years, Xamarin released Xamarin Studio, an open source IDE, and Xamarin.Forms (officially launched in 2014). Xamarin.Forms enabled developers to create XAML views that would work on different platforms. Xamarin, prior to Xamarin.Forms, had required developers to create separate views using the native platforms (Android XML layouts, iOS storyboards).

© Iris Classon 2025
I. Classon, *Migrating from Xamarin.Forms to .NET MAUI*,
https://doi.org/10.1007/979-8-8688-1215-6_1

Figure 1-1. *Xamarin's logo*

In 2016, Microsoft acquired Xamarin, integrating its technology and team into the Microsoft ecosystem. This acquisition brought several advantages, such as broader community support, more resources, stable funding, and better integration with existing tools, such as Visual Studio.

The announcement of .NET Multi-platform App UI (MAUI) came in 2020 as part of Microsoft .NET 6. .NET MAUI was envisioned as the evolution of Xamarin.Forms, aiming to create a more unified and streamlined framework for building cross-platform applications. Microsoft outlined a timeline for the end of support for Xamarin.Forms, setting a clear path for developers to transition to .NET MAUI, with the final support for Xamarin.Forms ending in May 2024.

Common Questions

As developers move from Xamarin.Forms to .NET MAUI, they often have questions about the changes, requirements, and advantages of the new framework. In this section, I'll be addressing the questions that I've come across the most.

Is MAUI a New Platform?

.NET MAUI is not a new platform, but rather an evolution of Xamarin.Forms. It builds on the foundation of Xamarin.Forms and adds improvements such as a more unified framework, more target platforms, improved performance, more flexible layouts, and various other enhancements.

Do I Have to Migrate?

Yes, migrating from Xamarin.Forms to .NET MAUI is necessary. Support for Xamarin.Forms ended in May 2024, meaning no further updates, bug fixes, or security patches will be provided. Apple will likely require Xcode 16 for new apps and updates by mid-2025, and Google Play is expected to require Android API level 35 or 36 by June 2025. Without migrating to .NET MAUI, you won't be able to publish new apps or update existing ones, as Xamarin.Forms won't meet these new platform requirements.

Is .NET MAUI Stable for Production Use?

Yes, it is. MAUI has been stable for a while, and the team continues to address issues and bugs. Several major apps are built with .NET MAUI, such as

- Vestas, a leading company in sustainable energy

- Microsoft Azure App

- NBC Sports Next

- Escola Agil, a Brazilian educational company

- The Postage, an end-of-life planning service

Do I Have to Rewrite Everything?

You don't have to rewrite everything when migrating to .NET MAUI. Business logic and non-UI code can mostly be left as is. However, some adjustments are necessary for UI code, particularly custom renderers and layout controls. There are some significant layout behavior changes, and we will cover those later in the book. The new single project structure is recommended in .NET MAUI, which means you'll have to consolidate platform-specific code into one project. This requires some reorganization of your current project setup.

Will My Current Xamarin Libraries and Plugins Work with .NET MAUI?

Many, but not all, third-party libraries support .NET MAUI, and the number is growing by the day. You could, depending on the license, migrate a library yourself, but chances are somebody has already done that. If not, look for alternatives.

What Are the Key Differences Between Xamarin and .NET MAUI?

Although .NET MAUI should feel familiar to Xamarin.Forms developers, there are some key differences. One of the biggest changes is the support for single project structure, which consolidates platform-specific code and resources into a unified project. This is a significant shift from Xamarin. Forms, which required a separate project for each platform. .NET MAUI provides a unified API that abstracts platform-specific details. Performance is greatly improved; we have Blazor integration, better data binding, richer controls, and Hot Reload. Although these are a handful of noteworthy differences, we will explore many more as we go further into the book.

Summary

For many cross-platform developers, .NET MAUI ticks all the boxes, but the most important box is future-proofing your application. What started as the Mono project evolved into Xamarin, then .NET MAUI, and today we have a framework that has been around for more than a decade. It has endured a great deal, and as is typical with open source projects, there are diverse viewpoints. With that said, this is not the only cross-platform framework out there, and in the next chapter, we will dive into .NET MAUI's features, compare it with alternatives, and address its future.

CHAPTER 2

.NET MAUI: Features, Alternatives, and Future

.NET MAUI isn't the only choice for cross-platform development, as there are other options available regardless of your preferred programming language or framework. My team thoroughly explored different options and had numerous in-depth discussions. In the end, we felt confident about our decision to use .NET MAUI. In this chapter, we will take a look at the features and improvements of .NET MAUI and examine different alternatives, such as Avalonia and Flutter. Last, we will discuss the future of .NET MAUI. By the end of this chapter, I hope you feel confident about your choice.

Features

Earlier in the book, I briefly touched upon some of the features and enhancements, but I haven't delved into them extensively. Let's examine those more closely.

© Iris Classon 2025
I. Classon, *Migrating from Xamarin.Forms to .NET MAUI*,
https://doi.org/10.1007/979-8-8688-1215-6_2

Single Project Structure

For some developers, this was a strong feature, but for others it was a pain. Although you can use a multi-project structure, in my experience, it wasn't worth it. My team never got it to work, as the build would break with missing internal assemblies. We could only find simple, naïve examples, and we weren't alone in struggling to make multi-project structure working for us. The single project structure is the default structure and therefore also the structure the MAUI team uses. Consequentially, this means that it is more extensively tested, and therefore, unless it's a complete deal breaker for you, I'd recommend using the single project structure. The benefits of the single project structure are mainly a simplified project setup, easier code sharing, less duplication, and fewer assemblies to manage. Additionally, some find it easier to navigate, but it does add more folder nesting.

Performance

Performance was one of the initial differences that we were absolutely thrilled about. It blew our mind away, particularly in build and simulator deployment time. I had gotten used to waiting a couple of minutes for the solution to build, deploy to the simulator or device, and painfully watch that splash screen slowly come into view. As soon as we got the app building with .NET MAUI, the app would be built and deployed in seconds.

Performance has been an important goal for the .NET MAUI team, and we've seen improvements right off the bat with the first release. One specific test, called LOLs per second, was used to measure page rendering performance. This test involves rendering a large number of labels with the text "LOL," each with random colors and rotations. In this test, .NET 7 MAUI showed a 51% improvement in page rendering speed compared to .NET 6 MAUI.

In addition to faster rendering, scrolling performance also improved significantly, with smoother scrolling and reduced GPU spikes, especially on lower-end Android devices. Figure 2-1 highlights these performance improvements, measured using the LOLs per second test.

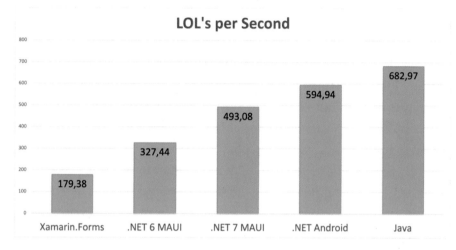

Figure 2-1. *LOLs per second measures the number of "LOL" labels per second. Performance has more than doubled from Xamarin. Forms to .NET 7 MAUI*

If you are a performance nerd, then I highly recommend reading the Performance Improvements in .NET blog posts by Stephen Toub found here: https://devblogs.microsoft.com/dotnet/performance-improvements-in-net-8/. The blog post is 16,000 words and approximately 56 pages, and he has written other performance blog posts. Don't miss out on the comments; they're really good, so give them a read.

Improved Abstractions

Besides performance, my second favorite improvement was more and better abstractions. With the launch of what was formerly referred to as .NET Core (.NET 5), Microsoft went all in with abstractions, best practices, and design patterns. For example, IoC (inversion of control) and DI (dependency injection) were incorporated into the framework, making it easier for developers to write maintainable and flexible code. This shift in mindset can be seen in Microsoft's newer frameworks, such as .NET MAUI. .NET MAUI has built-in support for dependency injection (DI), leveraging the same DI framework as ASP.NET Core, but it doesn't stop there. For example, .NET MAUI replaces custom renderers with unified handlers, which are more efficient and easier to implement. Platform-specific APIs are abstracted, allowing us to access platform-specific capabilities with a unified API call. You can also see this with UI elements. For example, I've spent more time getting a shadow just right, using custom renderers for the different platforms, than any human should use. I used to joke that the shadow literally, and metaphorically, followed me. With MAUI, it's as simple as using the shadow property on a control.

Hot Reload

Hot Reload in .NET MAUI enables real-time updates to the app's UI and logic without restarting the application. This feature significantly speeds up the development process by allowing developers to see changes instantly. It really makes UI work less painful and supports live debugging.

.NET MAUI's Hot Reload feature primarily supports XAML Hot Reload and does not support C# code reloading directly. This means that while you can make changes to your XAML code and see them reflected in real time without rebuilding the application, changes to C# code, such as event handlers, require a rebuild. Additionally, XAML Hot Reload supports simultaneous debugging of multiple platforms (using Visual Studio). However, separate head projects per platform is a requirement, rather than a single project app. Simultaneous debugging allows you to deploy your code to both Android and iOS devices simultaneously, so you can see the changes on both platforms at the same time.

Built-In Controls and Improved Layouts

While Xamarin.Forms already had a wide range of controls, .NET MAUI further expanded and enhanced the existing portfolio of controls. Here are some additions.

Border

In the past, I've used the Frame control and padding or a third-party library, but .NET MAUI includes a Border control that allows for easy customization.

GraphicsView

GraphicsView is a powerful control introduced in .NET MAUI that allows developers to draw custom graphics and create complex visuals within their applications. This control is particularly useful for scenarios where standard UI elements are insufficient, and custom drawing is required. Some key features are

- Custom drawing

- Animations

- Event handling

- Seamless integration with other controls

MenuBar and MenuBarItem

.NET MAUI introduces MenuBar and MenuBarItem for creating application menus, especially useful for desktop applications.

Shapes and Paths

Although added to Xamarin.Forms in 4.7, these have been optimized for better performance and integration.

CollectionView, CarouselView, and SwipeView

There have been significant enhancements made to the animations, resulting in a smoother experience. Likewise, the navigation controls have seen similar improvements.

View Shadow

MAUI views have a shadow property, which means we don't need to handle the shadow for the different platforms. However, I want to add that there have been a few issues with the shadow property, in particular with nested views. And at the time of writing, the shadow property renders differently on the different platforms. We've had to add handlers to set different shadow properties depending on the platform.

Other Noteworthy Improvements

There are more improvements beyond those I mentioned earlier, and I'm sure I've left out some of them by accident. The following is a concise list, though it is not extensive:

- Images in a single location

- Decoupled platform controls from cross-platform controls

- AppBuilder pattern (MauiAppBuilder) to standardize app bootstrapping with common .NET patterns

- Better desktop support

- Rebuilt layouts to fix bugs and performance issues

- Refactored Shell implementations

Managing image resources in .NET MAUI.

To streamline app development, you can specify images in one place within your project, and they will be automatically resized to the appropriate resolution for the target platform and included in the app package when building. Please note that .NET MAUI converts SVG files to PNG files. If you use SVG files, make sure you reference them with the .png extension in your views (regardless of whether it's XAML or C#).

Alternatives

Since I am not well-versed in the alternatives and there may be changes by the time you read this book, I will provide a brief overview of a few current options. I will discuss the advantages and disadvantages, but ultimately the direct comparison will be determined by you and your team since it depends on the specific requirements of the project. As an example, our team was enthusiastic about using Flutter, but the 15 .NET developers with extensive Xamarin.Forms experience would have to learn new tools, a new language, create a new pipeline, and a lot more. All of this would be prohibitively costly. It would be risky because we have product releases planned years in advance, and those deadlines are not flexible. Therefore, we cannot afford to be delayed for an extended period. While we were tempted by the idea of using something completely different and having fun with it, it could have potentially been an expensive experiment. .NET MAUI was for us the safest, fastest, and cheapest option.

.NET Alternatives

Being able to use the existing expertise of .NET developers on your team is a big plus, but .NET MAUI isn't the only .NET alternative. Let me provide you with a few options.

Uno Platform

Uno Platform allows you to build native mobile, desktop, and web apps with a single codebase using C# and XAML. It focuses on providing a consistent UI experience across all platforms.

Pros: Strong alignment with Microsoft's ecosystem, support for WinUI, and extensive platform coverage

Cons: Smaller community compared to .NET MAUI and sometimes lagging behind in support for the latest platform features

Avalonia

Avalonia is an open source, cross-platform UI framework for .NET, primarily targeting desktop applications but also supporting mobile.

Pros: Rich styling capabilities, support for MVVM, and a vibrant open source community

Cons: Still maturing in terms of mobile support and may lack some of the out-of-the-box integrations available in .NET MAUI

Non-.NET Alternatives

However, if your team is diverse or have the resources to embark on a completely new journey (or even take in new developers), then it might be worth looking into some non-.NET alternatives.

Flutter

This is the famous, and popular, Google's UI toolkit for building natively compiled applications for mobile, web, and desktop from a single codebase.

Pros: Fast performance, expressive and flexible UI, and a large community

Cons: Uses Dart instead of C#, which might require learning a new language for .NET developers

Ionic

This is a framework for building cross-platform mobile and web apps using web technologies like HTML, CSS, and JavaScript.

Pros: Familiar web development experience, extensive plugin ecosystem.

Cons: Performance may not be as high as native or other compiled frameworks.

Titanium

I had to give Titanium a mention, even though I'm not sure how up to date the framework is. Remember the App1 I mentioned at the start of the book? Well, when I ported my Windows Phone app to iOS, I used Titanium and Titanium Studio. Titanium is an older framework for building native mobile apps using JavaScript.

Pros: Long-standing presence in the market

Cons: Less active development and smaller community compared to newer frameworks

The Future of .NET MAUI

.NET MAUI has a bright future ahead, thanks to ongoing investments from both Microsoft and the open source community. While there may be skeptics, even negative feedback is highly valuable and actively contributes to the growth of this framework. I have personally submitted multiple issues to the repository and actively participated in discussions without hesitating to provide constructive criticism. While MAUI has a promising future, I understand the concerns and hesitations of some who fear it might meet the same fate as Silverlight, Windows Phone, and other technologies. One thing I am certain of is that the .NET MAUI team is fully committed to the framework. There is no evidence to suggest that this is a temporary project. On the contrary, the framework has experienced significant advancements and an increase in contributors and followers. The increasing adoption by well-known enterprises for large-scale .NET MAUI apps sends out a clear message: companies are willing to invest. The road maps are public and can be found on GitHub at `https://github.com/dotnet/maui/wiki/Roadmap`.

Release Schedule

.NET MAUI is released in sync with major .NET versions, typically following an annual release cadence. The major releases usually occur in November each year.

For example, .NET 6, .NET 7, and .NET 8 included updates and improvements to .NET MAUI. In addition, .NET MAUI receives monthly service updates, similar to the .NET platform, to address bug fixes, performance improvements, and new features.

Unlike .NET itself, .NET MAUI does not have Long-Term Support (LTS) versions, meaning each major release is supported for a minimum of six months after the next major version is released. To maintain support, developers need to upgrade to the latest major version within this period.

Summary

.NET MAUI is here to stay, and as the next step in the Xamarin.Forms evolution, it brings better performance, new and improved controls, simpler project structure, Hot Reload, and so much more to the table. However, there are .NET alternatives, such Avalonia, and non-.NET alternatives, such as Flutter. Only you and your team know what is the best fit, but .NET MAUI has long-term support, a public road map, and has been adopted by large enterprise companies. In other words, .NET MAUI is a robust solution for cross-platform development.

CHAPTER 3

Introducing the Case Study: A Fitness Application

In this chapter, I'll introduce the fitness application I built specifically for this book—*AppForFitness*. It's going to be our case study as we navigate the migration process from Xamarin.Forms to .NET MAUI. This app, designed to track One Rep Max (1RM) progress across different exercises, will help us explore the practical challenges and benefits of migrating a real-world application to MAUI.

Let's dive into what the app does, how it's structured, and what we need to keep in mind as we move to .NET MAUI.

Application Overview

At its core, AppForFitness helps users track their 1RM progress for various exercises, like the bench press, squat, and deadlift. The app fetches exercise data from an external API, caches the data, and displays user progress through interactive charts. The app securely stores local data and preferences such as app language, user information, and user preferences for the calculations. It's a simple, yet incomplete, fitness tool, with custom effects, deep linking, gesture-based interactions, and real-time localization.

© Iris Classon 2025
I. Classon, *Migrating from Xamarin.Forms to .NET MAUI*,
https://doi.org/10.1007/979-8-8688-1215-6_3

Application Pages Overview

The app is composed of several pages, each serving a specific purpose. These pages were designed to showcase migration challenges, but I've also aimed to make it function and behave like a fully working application. It features navigation, data visualization, and accessibility options, all of which are integral to a modern app experience. Below is a breakdown of each page and its functionality.

Main Page

The main page of the app provides users with quick access to the core functionalities. It uses a TabbedPage that lets the user navigate to key areas like progress tracking, entering new data, and adjusting settings. The navigation structure is built with a focus on ease of use, leveraging Xamarin's tabbed navigation.

Progress Page

The Progress page (Figure 3-1) is the app's core feature, allowing users to visualize their One Rep Max (1RM) progress across different exercises and muscle groups. Using OxyPlot to generate dynamic charts, users can

- View how their 1RM has progressed over time for various exercises.

- Switch between different 1RM formulas by long-pressing the chart, updating the data instantly.

- The charts retrieve data from an external API and plot it based on the selected exercise and muscle group.

- A Quick Add feature lets the user add an entry faster, by preselecting the exercise.

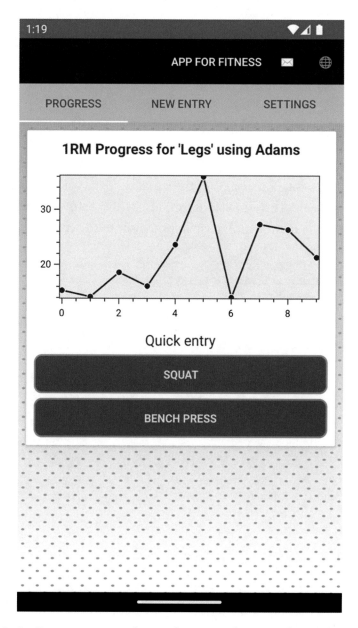

Figure 3-1. *Progress page shows the 1RM chart and Quick Add entries*

Entry Page

The Entry page (Figure 3-2) allows users to input new workout data. The user can access this page from the Quick Add or by clicking the tab for the page or by deep linking from an external source such as a website. Deep linking allows users to navigate directly to specific pages in the app from external sources, such as a website or an email. For example, a link like `http://appforfitness.com/entrypage?exerciseName=Squat` takes users directly to the Entry page for the squat exercise without needing to manually navigate. The app listens for these URLs, extracts parameters (like the exercise name), and navigates the user to the correct page.

Key features:

- Manually add new workout entries (exercise, weight, reps)

- Quickly select favorite exercises by clicking the workout icon

- Accessible directly from deep links, enabling users to add entries from external sources, like a website

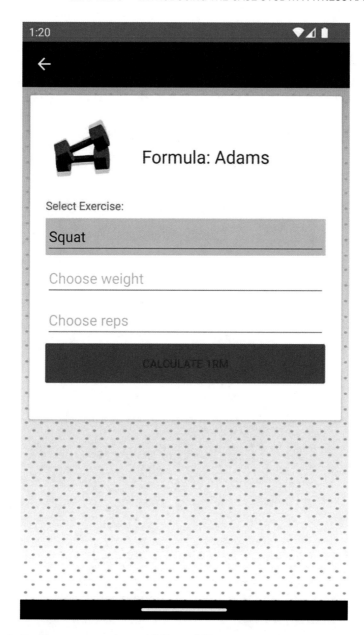

Figure 3-2. *Entry page is used for adding new entries*

Settings Page

The Settings page (Figure 3-3) gives users control over key app settings, for example, the default formula for 1RM. I've omitted other settings.

Key features:

- Set a default formula for calculating 1RM.

- Preferred formula is saved as a local user preference.

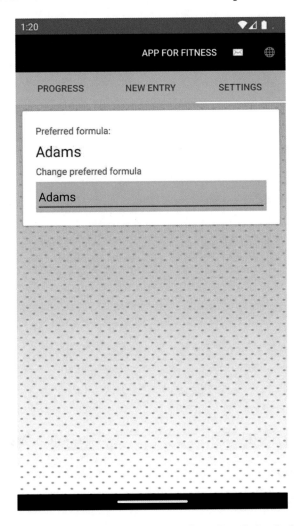

Figure 3-3. *Settings page lets the user select the default formula*

Language Selection Pop-Up

The Language Selection pop-up (Figure 3-4) is a custom pop-up built using a pop-up control. It allows users to choose the language they wish to use within the app. The app will update text dynamically when a new language is selected, without requiring a restart.

A little note on updating the text: I've only added localization to parts of the app to avoid adding too much code which would make it harder to follow the examples in the book.

Key features:

- Pop-up menu for selecting the app's language.

- Text updates when a new language is chosen.

- Preferred language is saved locally as a user preference.

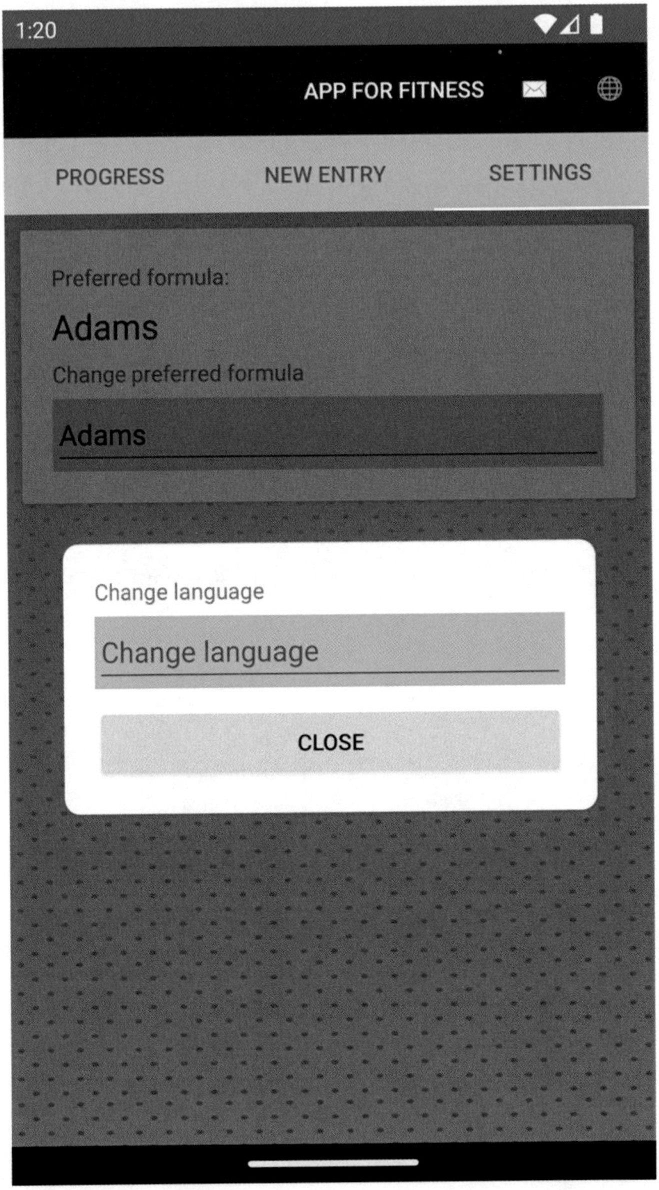

Figure 3-4. Language pop-up lets the user set the default language for the app

Email Pop-Up

The Email pop-up (Figure 3-5) is designed for direct interaction with users who need to provide feedback or request support.

Key features:

- Allows users to send emails directly from the app

- Opens the user's email client with a prefilled template for ease of use

- Simple, user-friendly pop-up for sending emails

- Integrates directly with the device's email application

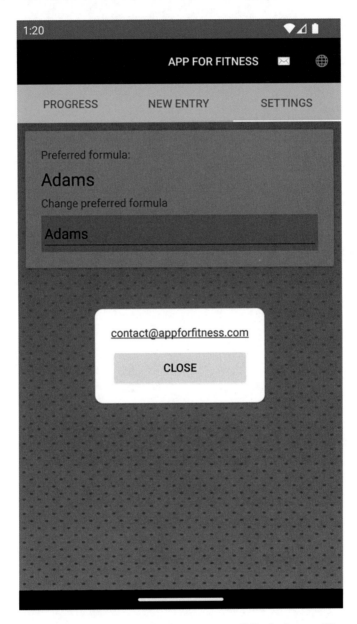

Figure 3-5. *Email pop-up contains an email link that will open the phone email app with prefilled template*

Application Structure

The application is a multi-project Xamarin.Forms solution, following the traditional structure with a shared library (Figure 3-6) and platform-specific libraries for Android and iOS (Figure 3-7). In this book, we'll focus more on Android as, in my experience, migrating Android apps has presented more challenges compared to iOS. This is also reflected in the number of bug reports filed in both the Xamarin.Forms and .NET MAUI repositories.

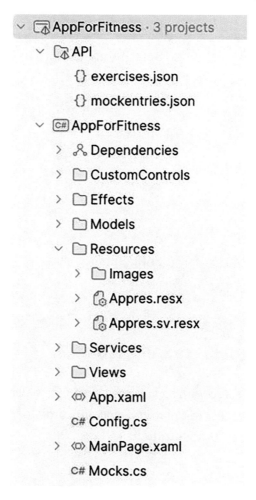

Figure 3-6. *Shared library structure*

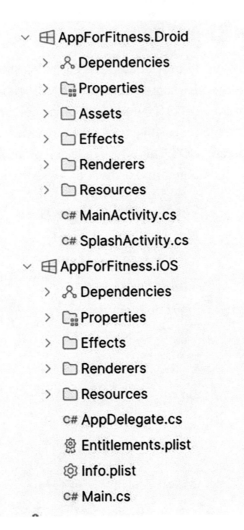

Figure 3-7. *Android and iOS project structure*

I structured the app with separation of concerns, using defined models, views, services, and platform-specific implementations to handle functionality across iOS and Android.

These are the main components:

- Data models: Models like Exercise, Lift, and LiftLogEntry define how data is organized. These models are key to ensuring we handle the user's workout data efficiently.

- Custom controls and effects: I've built controls such as the IconButton, LanguagePicker, and LongPressView to extend standard Xamarin.Forms components. Additionally, effects like ShadowEffect improve the user experience by adding visual depth to elements.

- Services and data handling: The ExerciseCatalogueCacheService manages API data, while the SecureStorageService ensures that sensitive information is stored securely.

- Platform-specific implementations: To ensure the app looks and behaves consistently across platforms, I've written custom renderers and platform-specific logic in Android and iOS projects. These will need special attention during the migration to ensure a smooth transition.

- Navigation and views: Pages like the MainPage, SettingsPage, and EntryPage form the core navigation structure.

Technical Features

The application was purposefully created to showcase specific challenges that arise during a migration from Xamarin.Forms to .NET MAUI. With this in mind, several features were incorporated to highlight both the complexities and the improvements that the migration process offers. Let's take a closer look at some of the aspects that we will revisit during the migration.

Charting with Third-Party Libraries

The app uses OxyPlot to generate interactive charts showing the user's 1RM progress. This was added so we can take a look at dealing with third-party dependencies. There are other libraries as well, such as SkiaSharp, Newtonsoft, and more. Some third-party libraries do not have .NET MAUI equivalent.

Navigation

Users can quickly log their most recent workout from the main screen by clicking a button. This is done by using the Navigation object. Navigation in .NET MAUI has changed (for the better).

Deep Linking

As mentioned earlier, the app supports deep linking, making it possible for users to navigate directly to specific pages from external sources. This is particularly useful for linking to the Entry page from the app's website or from other external content like blog posts. Deep linking is slightly different in .NET MAUI.

Localization

The app supports multiple languages, and users can change the language on the fly without restarting the app. .NET MAUI provides options to localization implementation.

MessagingCenter

Localization in the app is done through a LanguagePicker that sends messages via MessagingCenter to update localized strings throughout the app. MessagingCenter is deprecated in .NET MAUI.

Secure Data Storage

To ensure user data is safely stored, the app uses Xamarin.Essentials to manage secure storage for User ID. Other user-specific settings are stored with this library, which requires a migration to .NET MAUI.

Long-Press Gesture

The app uses long-press gestures to provide quick access to functionality, such as switching between 1RM formulas on the progress chart. We will use this to discuss gestures in .NET MAUI.

Accessibility and Semantic Properties

Accessibility is a crucial focus of the app, and several features are in place to ensure it's usable for all audiences. .NET MAUI has further improved this with SemanticProperties.

Styling and Themes

The app's UI is built with a resource dictionary, which defines global styles and colors for consistency. Although the app doesn't yet support theme switching (e.g., light/dark modes), the structure is in place for easy future updates. We will take a look at what has changed or improved in .NET MAUI.

Splash Screen Updates

Splash screen management has improved in MAUI, and I've included an example we can play with. MAUI allows for easier configuration of splash screens, especially for supporting multiple platforms.

Custom Shadow Effect

To add depth to UI components, I implemented a simple custom shadow effect. This effect enhances the visual experience and ensures key components stand out. Shadows are easier to deal with in .NET MAUI, and we'll take a look at that later.

Custom Renderers

The app has a couple of custom renderers which we'll use to discuss at the .NET MAUI equivalent, handlers. For example, we'll take a look at the app's custom image button that supports shadows for transparent images with irregular shapes. Custom renderers have for many been one of the pain points when migrating.

Custom Controls

In addition to the shadow effect, the app also features custom controls like a pop-up layout and a LanguagePicker. These components demonstrate how custom features can enhance the user experience and will be streamlined during the migration to MAUI.

Layouts

The app uses a mix of layouts, including StackLayout, RelativeLayout, and AbsoluteLayout. These layouts structure the UI but come with some migration considerations. We'll review these layouts during migration to ensure compatibility and optimize performance. MAUI also changes how layout properties like padding and margins are handled, which we'll update as needed.

Image Management

The app uses both embedded images and platform-specific resources which will be helpful for us when we look at image management in .NET MAUI.

32

A Note on Code Structure and Best Practices

If you take a look at the source code of the AppForFitness project, you'll probably notice something right away—the application doesn't exactly follow best practices or use the most popular design patterns. In fact, the app relies heavily on the dreaded code-behind pattern, something many developers aren't too fond of. You might be thinking, "Why not use MVVM or another separation pattern that would make the migration smoother?" Well, there's a reason for this approach.

In my experience, many real-world Xamarin applications that are now being migrated to .NET MAUI weren't necessarily written with perfect code structures from the start. They've evolved over time, and with that maturity comes technical debt—spaghetti code, quick fixes, older implementation patterns, and, yes, code-behind. It's common to see this in mature apps where new features are added on top of old foundations, often without taking the time to refactor or update the architecture.

Had I written this app using a clean MVVM pattern or other separation of concerns from the beginning, the migration would certainly have been easier. But that's not what many of you will be dealing with when migrating your own apps. I want to make sure we cover scenarios that reflect reality—where technical debt is a factor and where refactoring may be necessary as part of the migration process.

That being said, I don't want you to focus too much on the code itself. Remember, this is an example app with a specific purpose: to show the process of migrating to .NET MAUI. There are gaps in the implementation—missing exception handling, placeholder features, and the like—because the goal here is to demonstrate the before and after and highlight the challenges we face along the way.

Later in the book, we'll dive into some refactoring techniques and look at how you can improve your app's architecture as part of the migration. But for now, let's keep our focus on the migration itself and how .NET MAUI can help us clean up and modernize these kinds of projects.

Summary

The fitness application, *AppForFitness*, was created as a case study to guide the migration process from Xamarin.Forms to .NET MAUI. The app is designed to track a user's One Rep Max (1RM) progress across various exercises, fetching data from an external API and displaying interactive charts using OxyPlot. It also includes features like secure storage for user preferences, deep linking for direct navigation from external sources, and localization with dynamic language switching.

The app has several pages—Main, Progress, Entry, and Settings—that each serve a specific purpose for our migration walk-through.

From a technical standpoint, the app highlights key challenges and opportunities for improvement during migration. These include managing third-party dependencies, updating navigation patterns, and handling custom renderers. The app's use of different layouts, image management techniques, and effects like custom shadows ensures that we explore a wide range of migration scenarios, making it an ideal project to demonstrate the transition from Xamarin.Forms to .NET MAUI.

In the next chapter, we'll prepare for the migration process by setting up the development environment and assessing the current state of the application. We'll review third-party dependencies, ensure everything is up to date, and compile a checklist for a smooth migration.

CHAPTER 4

Preparing for Migration

Good preparation is key to a smooth migration, and taking the time to set things up correctly at the start can save a lot of headaches down the line. In this chapter, I'll walk you through the essential steps to get everything ready before diving into the migration process. We'll cover setting up your development environment for .NET MAUI, making sure your Xamarin. Forms project is using the latest version, and taking stock of your app's dependencies and native code.

As this book covers migrating from Xamarin.Forms, I'm assuming you have a working Xamarin.Forms development environment for your current app, but I will briefly cover the steps for setting up your environment and a remote Mac host in a Windows virtual machine (VM). We are going to use Visual Studio on Windows for parts of the migration. The reason is because there is a very helpful tool that we can use that has not been ported to Mac OS at the time of writing. This tool is .NET Upgrade Assistant, a tool that helps automate much of the migration process by analyzing your Xamarin. Forms project and making the necessary changes to convert it into a .NET MAUI project. Although this tool simplifies many steps, it's currently only available on Windows, which is why we'll be using a Windows VM alongside our Mac setup. Don't worry; we'll walk through the manual steps as well, ensuring you understand every part of the process.

© Iris Classon 2025
I. Classon, *Migrating from Xamarin.Forms to .NET MAUI*,
https://doi.org/10.1007/979-8-8688-1215-6_4

The book is for Xamarin.Forms to .NET MAUI migration, but if you have other project types, such as Xamarin.Android, Xamarin.iOS, iOS app extensions, or binding libraries (to name a few), please refer to the Microsoft documentation here: `https://learn.microsoft.com/en-us/dotnet/maui/migration`.

OpenGL and Xamarin.WatchOS

OpenGL has been removed from iOS, and if your app relies on OpenGL for rendering, you'll need to migrate to Metal, which is Apple's modern graphics API. .NET MAUI supports Metal natively for iOS, but this may require some code changes if you've been directly interacting with OpenGL in Xamarin.iOS.

Xamarin.WatchOS is not supported in .NET MAUI, so if your app includes WatchOS functionality, you will need to find an alternative solution. One option is to bundle Swift extensions within your .NET for iOS apps to support WatchOS functionality. While this requires some additional work, it ensures your app can continue to provide WatchOS features.

Development Environment Setup

As mentioned earlier, we will be doing parts of the migration with Visual Studio on Windows, but we will also be using Rider for those of you who prefer Rider for cross-platform development. I personally use both—Rider at work and Visual Studio for my own projects—and I find both of them to be excellent for cross-platform .NET development. Each has its own strengths, and by covering both, I hope to give you flexibility in how you approach the migration process. The Upgrade Assistant is not mandatory but simplifies the migration as it automates much of the migration process.

Mac Setup with JetBrains Rider

Here is a short summary for setting up Rider on your Mac:

1. Install Rider: `https://www.jetbrains.com/rider`.

2. Install .NET SDK: `https://dotnet.microsoft.com/en-us/download`.

3. Install Xcode through the App Store.

4. Install Android Studio: `https://developer.android.com/studio`.

5. Configure Android Studio in Rider: Preferences ➤ Build, Execution, Deployment ➤ Android SDK.

Windows Setup with Visual Studio

Here is a short summary for setting up Visual Studio on Windows. If you aren't on a Windows machine, go through the steps for setting up a VM using Parallels or other virtualization software (or cloud alternative). The steps for setting up a VM are described in the next section.

1. Install Visual Studio: `https://visualstudio.microsoft.com/downloads/`.

2. Modify your setup to include cross-platform development as shown in Figure 4-1.

3. Create a first project and accept the prompt to install missing tools.

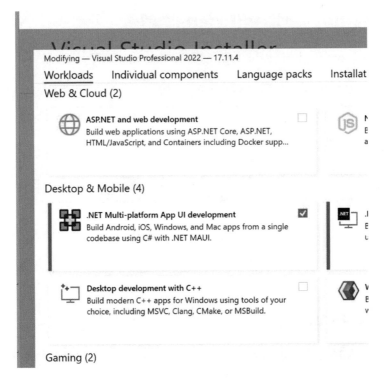

Figure 4-1. *Modify your Visual Studio installation to include the Desktop and Mobile development module*

Installing .NET MAUI

Setting up the environment for .NET MAUI is the same for both platforms as it can be done using the global dotnet tool which is installed with the dotnet SDK. .NET MAUI is installed as a workload.

A workload in the context of the .NET ecosystem refers to a set of tools, libraries, and SDK components required to build applications for specific platforms, such as mobile (iOS, Android), desktop (Windows, macOS), or web (Blazor). Workloads allow us to install only the platform-specific SDK components we need, making the .NET SDK modular and customizable.

Microsoft introduced the concept of SDK workloads to make the framework more flexible and lightweight. Instead of bundling all platform-specific libraries and tools into the base SDK, workloads enable us to selectively install the components necessary for our projects.

Use the command line to run the following:

```
dotnet workload install maui
```

When you run the command above, it installs the .NET MAUI workload and its associated tooling. By default, it includes support for all the target platforms that .NET MAUI supports: Android, iOS, macOS, and Windows.

However, to confirm that it is installed for all platforms, you can check for specific workload packs, such as

- maui-android

- maui-ios

- maui-maccatalyst

- maui-windows

These platforms should be installed automatically as part of the MAUI workload, but you can check by running

```
dotnet workload list
```

When you run a workload installation command for the first time, it will take a few minutes.

Setting Up a Windows VM

Setting up a VM is a straightforward process. Use a free trial account if you don't have a license for Windows or Parallels (unless you use free virtualization software).

1. Install a virtualization software, for example,
   Parallels: `https://www.parallels.com/` or
   VirtualBox (free): `https://www.virtualbox.org/`.

2. Download Windows ISO: `https://www.microsoft.com/en-us/software-download/windows11`.

3. Create a new virtual machine (the steps are similar
   for all virtualization software):

   a. Open Parallels and click Create New.

   b. Select the Windows ISO file or download directly from
      Parallels.

   c. Follow the on-screen instructions to complete the
      installation.

   d. Allocate resources, at least 8GB RAM and 100GB disk space.

Note   Keep in mind that if your virtual machine is on a different network, like when it is accessed remotely, you will have to set up a VPN in order to establish a connection between the Mac host and Windows VM.

Setting Up a Remote Mac Host

Microsoft has done a fantastic job integrating iOS and MacOS development in Visual Studio, and a remote host is configured in just a few steps.

1. On your Mac, enable Remote Login in settings here:
   Sharing ➤ Remote Login ➤ Enable. Click the info
   icon and write down the IP address.

2. Run the following command in your terminal to get the username for your Mac: whoami

3. In Visual Studio, select Tools ➤ iOS ➤ Pair to Mac (Figure 4-2) and select your Mac.

4. If your Mac is not on the list, confirm it's on the same network, and manually add the Mac by using the IP address from earlier (Figure 4-3).

5. Log in using the username and your Mac password.

6. Build and run the project from earlier, deploying to iOS.

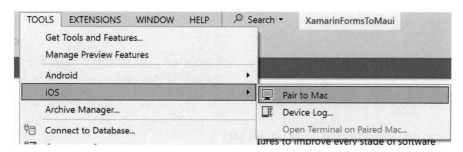

Figure 4-2. *Pair to Mac can be found under the Tools tab in the main menu*

Figure 4-3. *By default, your Mac should show up in the list. If you can't see it there, add it using the IP address from earlier*

Premigration Checklist

Before we begin the code inventory, there are a few foundational tasks we should complete to ensure a clean starting point for the migration. These steps shouldn't take long, and while steps 1 and 2 are not mandatory, I strongly recommend following them.

Step 1: Upgrade to the Latest Version of Xamarin.Forms

If you've already upgraded your project, please make sure you do indeed have the latest version of Xamarin.Forms.

Microsoft released an additional version of Xamarin.Forms 5.x after initially indicating that Xamarin.Forms would no longer receive major updates. This decision was likely made in response to developers needing more time to migrate their apps to .NET MAUI. The extra time allowed Microsoft to address remaining bugs and compatibility issues and ensure better support for developers who might not be ready to migrate immediately.

Another significant reason for this update was Apple's strict requirements. Apple regularly releases updates for iOS, macOS, and Xcode, and they enforce strict compatibility rules. Any app developed for iOS must be built with a recent version of Xcode to remain compliant with Apple's App Store policies (which is also why we have to migrate to .NET MAUI, if we want the app to run on iOS18). By upgrading to the latest version of Xamarin.Forms, your project will have improved compatibility with the latest versions of iOS, Android, and their respective SDKs, which will in turn make the migration to .NET MAUI easier.

Before you upgrade your NuGet packages, make sure that you have the appropriate version of Xcode:

1. Install command-line tools:

    ```
    xcode-select –install
    ```

2. Check the current version:

    ```
    xcodebuild -version
    ```

    If the version isn't 15.x, you have to manually download the version. If you update via App Store, you'll end up with version 16 or later, which will not work with Xamarin.Forms 5.x.

3. Go to the downloads in the developer portal: https://developer.apple.com/download/.

4. Search for Xcode 15.

5. Download the file, expand and unpack by double-clicking it, and give it a unique name.

6. Set the specific version as default:

```
sudo xcode-select --switch /Applications/
Xcode<version>.app
```

7. Check the version again:

```
xcodebuild -version
```

You can also set the Xcode version by setting the path for the Xcode version you want to use in Rider or Visual Studio.

Visual Studio: Tools ➤ Options ➤ Xamarin ➤ iOS Settings

Rider: Settings ➤ Build, Execution, Deployment ➤ Apple Platforms

In addition, get the latest versions of Android SDK for your IDE. If you are using Rider, then this can be done through the Android SDK Updater, found in the Preferences window: Preferences ➤ Languages and Frameworks ➤ Android SDK Updater.

In Visual Studio: Tools ➤ Android ➤ Android SDK Manager.

Build your solution, run any tests you might have, deploy the app, and verify the app starts without issues.

Step 2: Final Check

This step is crucial as we want to ensure the app is functioning perfectly and have a solid backup before proceeding with the migration.

1. Update dependencies:

    a. Check if other dependencies or NuGet packages used in your project have newer versions available.

    b. Update them where possible, and take note of any deprecated dependencies that may require refactoring later.

2. Exploratory Testing:

    a. Perform thorough exploratory testing across all platforms (iOS, Android, etc.), using both simulators and physical devices.

    b. Ensure that every feature and functionality works as expected.

    c. If any errors or issues arise during testing, fix them immediately and rerun the tests.

3. Back up the codebase:

    a. Version control: I strongly recommend using version control (such as Git, Bitbucket, GitHub, etc.). If you don't have it set up yet, now is the perfect time.

    b. Commit changes: Once you're confident that the app is updated and running as expected, commit the changes to your version control system.

    c. If you don't have version control in place, at the very least, create a manual backup of the entire codebase.

4. Test external entry points:

    a. Test deep links and other external entry points to make sure they behave correctly. The AppForFitness deep link can be tested by using the terminal:

    ```
    adb -s emulator-5556 shell am start -W -a android.
    intent.action.VIEW -d " https://irisclasson.github.
    io/AppForFitnessApi/entrypage?exerciseName=Squat"
    com.companyname.AppForFitness
    ```

    Use adb devices to get the right emulator:

    ```
    adb devices
    ```

You can also use this site, where we fetch the exercise catalog and other data. Click the button to get routed: `https://irisclasson.github.io/ AppForFitnessApi/`

5. Test the app's functionality. Pay special attention to custom controls and renderers to ensure they work without issues.

6. If your app uses Bluetooth, network connectivity, or requires permissions (e.g., for the camera or location services), make sure to test these scenarios thoroughly.

7. Don't forget to check for proper functioning of animations, as they can behave differently on different platforms or after updates.

By ensuring that everything works and is backed up, you'll minimize risks during the migration process and ensure you have a stable fallback in case anything goes wrong. I've had to learn this the hard way a few times; don't make the same mistake. It's better to commit and push often. Now, let's shift our focus to the inventory.

Step 3: Dependency and Native Code Inventory

This step is vital for migration preparation. Conducting a full inventory of your dependencies and native code allows you to plan the migration process effectively and anticipate challenges. The aim with this step is to

• Estimate work and resource (time and personnel) allocation.

- Identify major challenges. Some libraries might not have a MAUI equivalent or might need to be rewritten or removed. Knowing ahead of time means we can address this early on and allocate our time better.

- Avoid big surprises. While we cannot completely prevent unforeseen problems, we can make an effort to reduce them by being prepared.

- Identify code that would benefit from refactoring. If your inventory reveals significant technical debt or outdated patterns, you can make a note, and if time allows, address those during or before the migration.

- And last, let's not forget about the deployment pipeline. Documenting your dependencies and native code allows you to evaluate how the migration will impact your testing infrastructure and CI/CD pipelines. This book does not cover this aspect, as these pipelines vary wildly from project to project. I would like to point out that the retirement announcement of Microsoft App Center (used for analytics and crash reporting) had a direct impact on our pipeline. We also discussed maintaining two solutions side by side, which I'll get back to in the next chapter.

Taking Stock of Dependencies

Use a spreadsheet to track your findings, grouped by categories. For each line, add a column for MAUI compatibility, priority, action, version (if it's an external dependency), and so on.

Note   If the migration is urgent, keep the inventory succinct and don't delve too long on specific points. You will discover additional issues and maybe find out that some issues were non-issues, as you migrate, so don't let the inventory slow down the process too much. Two developers should be able to complete this task in less than half a day or maybe a full day, if there are some points that need to be discussed. Do take note of code that could be refactored but make it a lower priority if you are pressed for time.

You can use these categories as a starting point, but feel free to customize them to match the app's functionality:

- External dependencies (third-party libraries)
- Internal dependencies (any homegrown libraries or in-house code that might need updating for MAUI)
- Platform-specific code such as
  - Controls
  - Views
  - Renderers
  - Effects
  - Other
- Graphics/Resources (just list these)

Finding External Dependencies

You can pinpoint external dependencies by using the NuGet Package Manager, as well as in the project files where you might have assemblies added directly.

The NuGet window, in Rider or Visual Studio, shows explicitly added packages, as well as implicit dependencies. There are more than 50 implicit dependencies for this small app, so the list is going to be very long. Place emphasis on the direct dependencies and identify their usage locations.

In Rider, you can right-click a dependency and select Find Dependent Code (Figure 4-4), and in Visual Studio you can install ReSharper by JetBrains (use a free trial) to access the same feature.

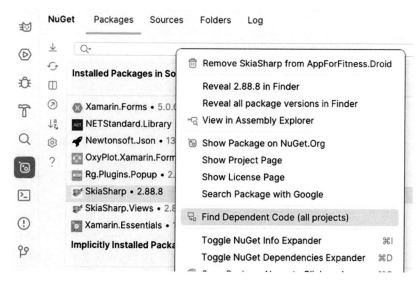

Figure 4-4. *Rider provides an option to finding dependent code for a package. ReSharper, by the same company, installed in Visual Studio will also give you access to this functionality*

In AppForFitness, we can see that we only use Newtonsoft for a single line of code (Figure 4-5), and SkiaSharp is only used to resize a bitmap which can be done with Xamarin.Forms libraries (Figure 4-6).

Don't forget to revert changes afterward!

Figure 4-5. *AppForFitness references the Newtonsoft package, but uses it for a single line of code that can be replaced by .NET libraries*

Figure 4-6. *SkiaSharp is used to resize a bitmap but doesn't require custom parameters that do not exist in the built-in resize function for the .NET bitmap object*

However, OxyPlot doesn't have the Find Dependent Code option, but we know it is used for the progress chart. Another way to check dependency usage is to remove the dependency and try to build. Follow the errors, and you'll find the usage.

You can see the dependency spreadsheet for AppForFitness in Table 4-1.

Table 4-1. *AppForFitness dependencies*

Category	Dependency	Version	MAUI Compatible	Action	Priority
External	Xamarin.Forms	5.0.0.2012	Sort of	Upgrade to .NET MAUI	High
External	NETStandard. Library	2.0.3	Yes	Upgrade to .NET 6	High
External	Newtonsoft. Json	13.0.3	Yes	Compatible. Can be replaced with System.Text.Json	Low
External	OxyPlot. Xamarin.Forms	2.1.0	No (needs migration)	Find alternative	High
External	Rg.Plugins. Popup	2.1.0	No (needs migration)	Not being used	High
External	SkiaSharp	2.88.8	Yes	Compatible, but can be replaced with own code	Low
External	SkiaSharp. Views	2.88.8	Yes	Compatible. See above	Low
External	Xamarin. Essentials	1.8.1	Yes	Included in .NET MAUI	Medium

It may not seem like a significant number, but eight dependencies are essential for the AppForFitness app to work effectively. However, in larger, more complex applications, you're likely to have many more dependencies. For example, in the Plejd app that my team and I work on, we have 22 dependencies—and that's after a lot of effort to keep the number low. We also have over 150 implicit dependencies, which means that even though the visible list of dependencies isn't overwhelming, there's a lot more happening under the surface.

When we migrated to .NET MAUI, most of these dependencies had a version that supported MAUI, but we took the opportunity to clean up our code and reduce the number of dependencies where possible. This is an important consideration: Even if your dependencies are supported, do you really need all of them? Reducing dependency complexity now can save you headaches in the future.

One example from our migration experience was the Microsoft AppCenter SDK that I mentioned earlier. Although they released a version that supports .NET MAUI, they also announced that AppCenter will be deprecated on March 31, 2025. This means that while .NET MAUI support is crucial, you also need to think about the long-term maintenance of the libraries you rely on. Major factors to take into account when choosing dependencies are the absence of ongoing bug fixes, security updates, and the possibility of deprecation.

Even if you're pressed for time and can't immediately refactor out unnecessary dependencies during migration, it's important to revisit your dependency inventory periodically. Use your spreadsheet as a living document to track dependencies, mark potential issues, and plan for future cleanups.

Internal Dependencies

When doing the inventory, don't forget to analyze homegrown libraries or in-house code that might need updating for .NET MAUI. While AppForFitness doesn't have any additional internal libraries, my experience with the Plejd app has shown that internal dependencies can often present unique challenges.

In Plejd, we use several internal libraries, some of which are managed by other teams. For example, the test team manages a library that defines constants used in our automated UI tests. This kind of internal dependency can be just as crucial to a successful migration as third-party libraries. If your app relies on internal libraries, you'll need to ensure that they are either updated for .NET MAUI or compatible with the new platform.

Internal dependencies may be added in different forms:

- Binaries: Precompiled libraries included in your project.

- Sub Git Submodules: Shared code repositories that are linked into your main project.

- A Git Subtree allows you to include one repository (your internal library) inside another repository (your main app) while still treating the internal repository as a separate entity. Unlike a submodule, a subtree copies the internal library into the main project.

- Shared projects: Projects that are shared across projects.

- Linked files: Files that are added as a direct link in several projects.

- NuGet packages from a private feed: Libraries packaged and distributed through an internal NuGet server.

- Build artifacts: Artifacts added to the project or app as a part of the build process.

When handling internal dependencies, communication across teams is important. Make sure that each team responsible for these libraries is aware of the migration and the timelines so that they can plan to update their code accordingly.

Platform-Specific Code

As mentioned earlier, when migrating to .NET MAUI, it's important to assess your app's platform-specific code and decide what to keep, refactor, or eliminate. The good news is that MAUI brings more cross-platform features, reducing the need for custom code per platform. However, some existing implementations, like custom renderers and platform-specific views, will still need attention.

53

Custom Renderers and Effects

In .NET MAUI, the concept of renderers has changed, evolving into something called handlers. This change simplifies the process of customizing platform-specific components while giving developers more flexibility. I'll cover the specifics of handlers in the next chapter. Overall, while platform-specific functionality is easier to manage in MAUI, there's still work involved in migrating existing renderers and effects.

From my experience, developers find that they need fewer custom renderers after migrating. Most of the work typically involves tweaking layouts and adjusting how custom controls are handled during the migration.

Custom Views and Controls

As with renderers, you'll likely find that you need fewer platform-specific views and controls in MAUI. The framework has added many cross-platform capabilities, meaning that some of the custom views you built for each platform in Xamarin.Forms may now be unnecessary in MAUI. This results in cleaner and more maintainable code, with fewer platform-specific dependencies.

Resources

One of the improvements in .NET MAUI is that sharing resources, such as images, across platforms has become much easier. With the new framework, you'll likely need fewer platform-specific resources. However, it's still important to include resources in your inventory, even if they don't require as much attention as other components.

When documenting resources, focus on where they are located and how they are accessed in your project (e.g., whether they are embedded resources, platform-specific images, or shared resources). You don't need to spend too much time on specifics at this stage, but it's helpful to note their paths and usage patterns to ensure they migrate smoothly.

Inventory Spreadsheet for Platform-Specific Code

You can use the following command in bash to get the tree structure of your project, excluding bin and obj folders and their children:

```
\tree -I 'bin|obj'
```

On Windows, you can use PowerShell and the following function:

```
function Show-Tree {
    param (
        [string]$Path = ".",
        [int]$Depth = 0
    )

    $indent = "    " * $Depth
    $items = Get-ChildItem -Path $Path | Where-Object
    { $_.Name -notmatch 'bin|obj' }

    foreach ($item in $items) {
        if ($item.PSIsContainer) {
            Write-Host "$indent|-- $($item.Name)"
            Show-Tree -Path $item.FullName -Depth ($Depth + 1)
        } else {
            Write-Host "$indent|-- $($item.Name)"
        }
    }
}
Show-Tree
```

You'll find a summary of the platform-specific code inventory for AppForFitness in Table 4-2.

Table 4-2. *Spreadsheet detailing the result of the platform-specific code inventory*

Category	Component	Current Usage	MAUI Equivalent	Action	Priority	Notes
Custom Control	IconButton	All platforms	Use MAUI Handlers	Refactor to handler	High	Layout adjustments may be needed
Custom Control	LanguagePicker	All platforms	Use MAUI Handlers	Refactor to handler	High	Layout adjustments may be needed
Custom Control	LongPressView	All platforms	Use MAUI Handlers	Refactor to handler	Medium	Ensure gestures work
Custom Control	PopupLayout	All platforms	Use MAUI Handlers	Refactor to handler	Medium	Ensure layout compatibility
Custom Effect	LoggingEffect	iOS, Android	Replace with MAUI built-in	Replace	Medium	Not being used. Can be removed
Custom Effect	ShadowEffect	iOS, Android	Replace with MAUI built-in	Replace	Medium	Simplify with MAUI shadow effect

Custom Renderer	IconButtonRenderer	iOS, Android	Use MAUI Handlers	Refactor to handler	High	Layout adjustments
Custom Renderer	LongPressViewRenderer	iOS, Android	Use MAUI Handlers	Refactor to handler	High	Ensure gesture handling
Custom Renderer	TabbedPageRenderer	iOS, Android	Use MAUI Handlers	Refactor to handler	High	Adjust for TabbedPage changes. Android version is empty. Can be removed for Android
Embedded Resource (Image)	bg.png	All platforms	Shared Resource	Add to shared folder	Low	Verify for cross-platform compatibility
Embedded Resource (localization)	Appres.resx	All platforms	Shared Resource	No action needed	Low	Standard localization file

(continued)

57

Table 4-2. (*continued*)

Category	Component	Current Usage	MAUI Equivalent	Action	Priority	Notes
Resource (image)	dumbell.png	iOS, Android	Replace with shared resource	Replace with shared resource	Medium	Same image on both platforms. Can be shared
Service	DeepLinkingService	All platforms	No change needed	No action needed	Low	Update for MAUI compatibility
Service	ExerciseCatalogueCacheService	All platforms	No change needed	No action needed	Low	Cache management is platform independent
Service	SecureStorageService	All platforms	No change needed	No action needed	Low	Secure storage integration works cross-platform
Service	FitnessApiService	All platforms	No change needed	No action needed	Low	API integration
Service	PermissionService	All platforms	No change needed	No action needed	Low	Permission management

Column Breakdown

- Category: What type of platform-specific element are you dealing with? Is it a custom renderer, custom effect, platform-specific control, or a resource (like an image or font)?

- Component: The name or type of the specific element in question (e.g., a custom renderer, image file).

- Current usage: Which platforms are currently using this code or resource? Is it Android specific, iOS specific, or used across all platforms?

- MAUI equivalent: What is the corresponding element or feature in .NET MAUI? This could be MAUI Handlers, built-in effects, or new cross-platform capabilities.

- Action: What action is required for this component? Do you need to refactor, remove, or replace it? This helps prioritize your work.

- Priority: Rank the priority of the migration for this element (High, Medium, Low). This helps allocate effort where it's most needed.

- Notes: Any additional notes or context for the component, such as potential layout adjustments or any platform-specific quirks.

How to Use the Spreadsheet:

1. List all your platform-specific elements (custom renderers, views, effects, and resources).

2. Identify MAUI equivalents for each component. I've added information regarding whether I can remove, refactor, or replace them. You might not have this information yet, but the spreadsheet isn't final. You'll add as you go.

3. Prioritize actions to ensure that high-priority tasks are handled first, such as critical renderers or views.

4. Track resources (images, fonts, etc.), noting their location. Later, you'll add information regarding whether they can be shared or if they need adjustment for MAUI.

App Navigation

Navigating between pages and views has evolved with .NET MAUI, and understanding these changes is essential for a smooth migration from Xamarin.Forms. So make sure to document how navigation is implemented within your app, highlighting the use of built-in navigation, custom navigation, and deep linking.

As before, use a spreadsheet. As an example, here is the navigation in AppForFitness. Use the IDE Find Usages feature (Table 4-3) to find usages of the type Navigation.

Table 4-3. *Spreadsheet overview of the navigation used in the app*

Page/View	Navigation Type	Params (Yes/No)
MainPage	Tabs	No
ProgressPage	Built-in (NavigationPushAsync)	Yes
EntryPage	Built-in (NavigationPushAsync)	No
LanguagePopup	Custom (Popup)	No
EmailPopup	Custom (Popup)	No
EntryPage	Deep Link with Built-in (NavigationPushAsync)	Yes

Summary

We've now set up our environment, so we can use Visual Studio on Windows to access a platform-specific migration tool, and we've also updated our project to the latest version of Xamarin.Forms. Additionally, we conducted a comprehensive inventory of our code, creating spreadsheets with detailed information on what needs to be addressed both before and during the migration process. In the next step, we'll plan the migration using the insights gathered in this chapter and finalize our overall migration strategy.

CHAPTER 5

Planning Your Migration

With the data we collected in the previous chapter, we will strategically plan our migration in this chapter, considering different approaches to project structure and deciding between a complete or incremental migration.

By thoroughly examining the main disparities between Xamarin. Forms and .NET MAUI, we will be ready to transition smoothly to the next chapter, where we will initiate the migration process with some minor cleanup addressing some of the easy-to-fix findings from our inventory.

Migration Strategies

When you migrate to .NET MAUI, you can either do a full migration or an incremental migration where you only migrate specific platforms. For example, iOS is the most urgent migration due to the reasons I mentioned at the start of the book. Android, on the other hand, has for many been more challenging to migrate (mostly due to UI differences), and I know several companies that kept Xamarin.Forms for Android and focused on iOS first.

© Iris Classon 2025
I. Classon, *Migrating from Xamarin.Forms to .NET MAUI*,
https://doi.org/10.1007/979-8-8688-1215-6_5

Full Migration vs. Incremental Migration

Incremental migration, in this context, refers to migrating selectively for certain platforms while maintaining Xamarin.Forms for the others (for now).

Incremental migration is often seen as beneficial because it allows for gradual testing of each step, makes it easier to maintain feature parity during the migration, and allows for allocation of only a portion of team resources, potentially avoiding a feature freeze. However, the Xamarin. Forms to .NET MAUI situation is different from other migration processes where the framework you are migrating from is still being developed or maintained. Support for Xamarin.Forms ended May 1, 2024, after adding a final last-minute release. In that release, by adding support for Xcode 15 and Android API 34, Microsoft enabled Xamarin to build against these specific SDK versions. However, it's important to note that Xamarin does not offer support for any new APIs introduced in these SDK versions. For Android 15 (API level 35) and up and for Xcode 16 and up, you need .NET MAUI. Android maintains a strong level of backward compatibility, meaning that older apps targeting previous API levels can still run on newer Android versions. If your Xamarin app targets a lower Android API, it could still run on newer Android devices. However, some features and behaviors may not work as expected due to changes in the Android system, deprecated APIs, and so on. For those reasons, I'd recommend migrating both platforms.

.NET MAUI Supported Platforms

I'd like to delve deeper into the topic of versions. Migrating to .NET MAUI impacts your app's support for legacy versions for the targeted platforms.

At the time of writing, .NET MAUI apps can be written for the following platforms:

- Android 5.0 (API 21) or higher is required.

- iOS 11 or higher is required.

- macOS 11 or higher, using Mac Catalyst.

- Windows 11 and Windows 10 version 1809 or higher, using Windows UI Library (WinUI) 3.

Moreover, if you decide to incorporate Blazor along with. NET MAUI (more information will be provided later in this chapter), you will have extra criteria to fulfill:

- Android 7.0 (API 24) or higher is required.

- iOS 14 or higher is required.

- macOS 11 or higher, using Mac Catalyst.

MacOS and Universal Windows Platform (UWP)

I haven't touched upon other platforms much as we are focusing on the two major platform targets, iOS and Android, in this book, but I do want to mention MacOS and UWP.

As with Android, there is better backward compatibility, but also the same issue of missing out on newer features. In addition, if your app is distributed through the Mac App Store, there are minimum SDK requirements for apps to remain listed. Apple may enforce using certain features (like supporting Apple Silicon architecture or integrating sandboxing). Not updating your Xamarin.Mac app might lead to its removal from the Mac App Store.

Project Structure

One of the significant changes in .NET MAUI is the introduction of multitargeting. Unlike Xamarin.Forms, where you had separate projects for each platform (e.g., iOS, Android), .NET MAUI allows for a single unified project structure that simplifies cross-platform development by reducing duplication. This approach was initially the recommended project structure, as seen in most sample apps, official documentation, and Microsoft's educational videos.

However, this change posed challenges for many developers, especially those with complex apps, who were used to the multi-project structure of Xamarin.Forms. The unified structure led to pushback from parts of the community, with many developers preferring the flexibility of having separate projects for each platform alongside a shared project. In response, Microsoft eventually added support for a multi-project structure, making it easier to maintain the old Xamarin.Forms setup.

When .NET MAUI first launched, we tried the multi-project structure in .NET MAUI as it translated better coming from our current app. But it was a pain, and we ended up spending more time than I'd like to admit trying to make the multi-project structure work. Our biggest challenge was related to missing build targets for Android, especially around AOT (Ahead-of-Time compilation), even after attempting to disable it.

Fortunately, a lot has changed since then. The multi-project template added later is much more stable and widely used by many developers today. It allows for greater flexibility, especially for those who want to stick to the multi-project structure. For many developers, especially those with large, complex apps or specific needs, the multi-project setup offers greater separation between platforms, making it easier to manage platform-specific resources, custom renderers, or third-party dependencies that differ by platform.

In this book, I'll be using the single project structure when we migrate, to demonstrate the difference and showcase how the unified project structure simplifies management for most apps. While I've personally been tempted to recommend this approach to all developers, especially because the single project structure received more attention and "love" early on in the MAUI lifecycle, it's not always the best fit for every app.

Major Differences and How to Address Them

Let's have a closer look at some of the bigger differences, how they affect us and how we address them. This is not an exhaustive list, but I've done my best to focus on what's most noticeable.

Project Structure

Xamarin.Forms uses a multi-project structure, where you typically have separate projects for each platform (Android, iOS, UWP, etc.). In contrast, .NET MAUI introduces a single project structure, which centralizes platform-specific code and resources in a single location. This reduces duplication and simplifies the project setup.

You can still use a multi-project structure in MAUI if preferred, but migrating to the single project format could simplify resource management and builds. Use multitargeting in .NET MAUI to include platform-specific resources in the shared project using folders like Platforms/Android, Platforms/iOS, etc.

Design Patterns

Built in to the .NET MAUI framework, you'll see examples of design patterns that are also extensively used in ASP .NET Core and other newer .NET frameworks. These patterns offer more flexible, scalable, and maintainable codebases. Here are some.

Dependency Injection (DI)

DI is now a first-class citizen in .NET MAUI. The DI container is integrated with the application's startup and lifecycle via MauiProgram.cs, similar to how it works in ASP.NET Core. If you already use DI, you can migrate your dependency resolution code without much hassle.

Handler Pattern

We'll cover this in more detail further down, but custom renderers are replaced with Handlers, using the handler pattern, which allow more modular and flexible customization of platform-specific control behavior.

Handlers can also be extended or replaced using something called mappers.

Builder Pattern

The builder pattern is extensively used, particularly in configuring the MauiApp. It follows the familiar App.CreateBuilder() pattern seen in ASP.NET Core for setting up services, middleware, and platform-specific configurations. It centralizes your service registrations, configurations, and platform specific.

Service Pattern

In .NET MAUI, the service pattern is where services (e.g., LocationService, NotificationService) are injected into your pages and ViewModels, further decoupling UI from logic.

These are just some of the many design patterns .NET MAUI has made first-class citizens, following the pattern (pun intended) we see overall for newer .NET frameworks.

UI Differences

When upgrading to .NET MAUI, one of the biggest changes is how layouts and controls behave compared to Xamarin.Forms. Some layout behaviors have changed, and default values for spacing and padding have been adjusted, as well as internal logic. Here's a breakdown of the major difference.

Layout Behavior Changes from Xamarin.Forms

In .NET MAUI, layout behavior has been improved to ensure that sizing requests are honored more consistently. Some changes in layout behavior might cause your existing Xamarin.Forms layouts to behave differently in MAUI.

Default Layout Value Changes

In Xamarin.Forms, default values for certain properties like padding, margins, and spacing were somewhat arbitrary. In .NET MAUI, the default values have been set to zero, leading to potential layout changes if explicit values aren't set. To preserve the Xamarin.Forms default values in projects that don't set explicit values, add implicit styles to your project. For more information about implicit styles, see Implicit styles.

Frame

In Xamarin.Forms, Frame controls had inconsistent behavior across platforms, especially when it came to measuring padding. In .NET MAUI, Frame has been replaced with Border, which offers consistent measurement across all platforms. However, Frame is still supported for migration purposes. Consider transitioning to Border, and use styles to adjust padding and behavior.

Grid

The biggest change in Grid is that .NET MAUI does not infer columns or rows as Xamarin.Forms did. You now have to explicitly declare ColumnDefinitions and RowDefinitions.

StackLayout

In .NET MAUI, StackLayout now behaves more predictably. It will stack child elements until all have been added, even if it exceeds the available space. In Xamarin.Forms, StackLayout sometimes expanded or stopped based on available space. .NET MAUI also introduces VerticalStackLayout and HorizontalStackLayout, and Microsoft recommends that you use those instead of defaulting to StackLayout. For layouts that need to subdivide space, use Grid. Properties *AndExpand (e.g., FillAndExpand) are ignored in VerticalStackLayout and HorizontalStackLayout, hence the Grid recommendation.

RelativeLayout

.NET MAUI discourages the use of RelativeLayout, which can only be used if you include the Microsoft.Maui.Controls.Compatibility package. Whenever possible, opt for using a Grid instead.

ScrollView

In .NET MAUI, the ScrollView automatically expands to fit its content unless you set specific constraints. This can be tricky for Xamarin.Forms users because, in a VerticalStackLayout—which can grow indefinitely— the ScrollView will stretch to the full height of its content and won't allow scrolling. We had quite a few issues with ScrollView when we migrated, so take note if your app uses ScrollView.

Cross-Platform Device APIs

Xamarin.Essentials is now integrated into .NET MAUI, allowing for seamless access to device APIs such as geolocation, sensors, and secure storage across platforms. This means one less package to keep track of.

Fonts, Images, and Resource Management

In .NET MAUI, resources such as fonts, images, and styles are managed centrally in the shared project. Although you probably already centralized a lot of the resource management in a shared project, .NET MAUI allows for more shared resources. In addition, resources such as fonts and more can be registered in the builder. We'll get back to this during the migration.

Accessibility

.NET MAUI improves accessibility with better support for Semantic Properties, which help make your app more accessible across platforms. There's also a namespace change, which is an easy fix when we migrate.

Localization

Localization in .NET MAUI has been simplified. All resource files (.resx) are centrally located in the shared project, and MAUI provides better support for switching languages dynamically by using the CultureInfo API to dynamically switch between languages.

Animations and Transitions

MAUI introduces more efficient and streamlined APIs for animations and transitions, allowing for smoother performance across platforms.

Custom Gesture Recognizers and Handlers

In cases where you need highly custom gestures (e.g., multi-touch gestures, drawing apps, etc.), .NET MAUI provides more flexibility in defining custom gesture recognizers or extending the built-in gesture handling system.

In Xamarin.Forms, creating custom gesture recognizers required implementing custom renderers to handle platform-specific touch or gesture inputs. This meant writing platform-specific code for iOS and Android, making it harder to create cross-platform solutions. If you wanted custom gestures beyond the built-in options (e.g., Tap, Pinch, Pan), you had to override native gesture recognizers in each platform's renderer. With handlers, gesture recognizers are now more cross-platform by default, and you can attach gesture recognizers directly to elements using the handler architecture. This removes the need for platform-specific code in most cases. Handlers also expose gesture APIs in a way that can be customized globally or conditionally for different platforms without diving into native code as often. We'll cover this in detail later in the book.

Performance

.NET MAUI brings significant performance improvements, especially with AOT (Ahead-of-Time) compilation and optimized startup times. AOT improves

- Startup performance: Because the code is already compiled into native code, there's no need for JIT compilation, which significantly reduces the time it takes for your app to launch.

- Memory usage: AOT can reduce memory consumption since runtime compilation structures aren't necessary.

- Battery life: With more efficient native execution, AOT reduces CPU load and power consumption, making apps more battery-efficient, which is crucial for mobile users.

There's also an improvement to garbage collection, reduced memory overhead, and better utilization of hardware.

Hot Reload and Hot Restart

Both Hot Reload and Hot Restart have been improved in .NET MAUI, allowing for faster debugging and testing. Use Hot Reload to update XAML and C# code without rebuilding and Hot Restart to test changes on physical devices without needing a full deployment. This is by far my favorite improvement, as deploying to Android would take up to four minutes. Most of our UI, in contrast to the AppForFitness app, is in C# and not XAML, and we had to deploy often.

.NET MAUI introduces several startup time optimizations to ensure your apps launch faster. This is how startup time is improved:

- Trimmed assemblies: .NET MAUI automatically trims unused assemblies and removes unnecessary metadata at compile time, reducing the overall size of your app. This is an opt-in feature, and there are some known limitations, for example, reflection-based serializers such as Newtonsoft (which we are able to replace based on our inventory), runtime code generation via JIT, dynamic assembly loading, and some platform-specific limitations for WPF and Windows Forms.

- Linker optimizations: The .NET Linker strips out unused code, resulting in smaller binaries and faster startup times. This needs to be explicitly set for application and can effect debugging experience.

- Lazy initialization: .NET MAUI supports lazy initialization, which means that certain services and libraries are only loaded when they are needed, instead of being initialized at app startup.

Summary

The fifth chapter concludes our journey before we commence our migration. In this chapter, we've outlined our migration strategy, focusing on the choice between complete and incremental migrations and project structure. We discussed key differences between Xamarin.Forms and .NET MAUI, especially in terms of project structure, UI behavior, lifecycle management, and device APIs. We explored design patterns that have been made first-class citizens and reviewed the changes in layout behavior and resource management in MAUI. Additionally, we covered performance improvements, such as Ahead-of-Time (AOT) compilation, trimmed assemblies, and linker optimizations that enhance app performance.

In the next chapter, we'll address some of the findings from our inventory, introduce the .NET Upgrade Assistant, and kick off the migration process with a focus on project structure, UI migration, and platform-specific integrations.

CHAPTER 6

Executing the Migration

We've finally arrived at the core part of the book—the migration! With all the preparation we've done, the migration should proceed smoothly, though some additional cleanup is still needed. In this chapter, we'll go through some minor refactoring opportunities before using the .NET Upgrade Assistant.

Terminology

To ensure clarity and consistency, we'll refer to the various projects as follows:

- Shared project: The Xamarin.Forms shared project that contains cross-platform logic but no platform-specific code. This project is where most of the non-platform-specific business logic, UI, and services reside.

- Android platform project: The Xamarin.Forms project that contains Android-specific resources and code. It manages platform-specific integrations, services, and resources related to Android (e.g., MainActivity, AndroidManifest.xml).

© Iris Classon 2025
I. Classon, *Migrating from Xamarin.Forms to .NET MAUI*,
https://doi.org/10.1007/979-8-8688-1215-6_6

- iOS platform project: The Xamarin.Forms project that contains iOS-specific resources and code. It handles iOS-specific implementations, such as AppDelegate, Info.plist, and other platform-dependent services.

- Migrated shared project: The migrated version of the shared project, which serves as an intermediary project during migration. This project will eventually be discarded after the migration is complete.

- Main MAUI project: The final .NET MAUI project where all code, including both shared and platform-specific resources and logic, will reside. This project includes platform folders (like Platforms/Android and Platforms/iOS) for platform-specific code, creating a unified project structure.

Additionally, while the Upgrade Assistant refers to the process as an upgrade, we'll continue to use the term migrate throughout this book. This is to stay consistent and clear in our intent, as the process involves significant restructuring and platform changes, not just a simple version upgrade.

Cleaning Up Before Migration

I cannot stress enough the significance of starting with the cleanest codebase possible. If you're pressed for time, you might need to leave some cleanup for later, but we've identified a few minor refactoring opportunities in the inventory chapter that we'll address here:

- Newtonsoft is only used for one line:

  - We can replace it with System.Text.Json, which will reduce dependencies.

- This allows us to enable performance features like trimming assemblies, which doesn't work well with reflection-based serializers like Newtonsoft.

- SkiaSharp is only used for image resizing:

  - Since we're not using advanced features or performance optimizations, we can achieve image resizing with built-in libraries, making SkiaSharp unnecessary.

- LoggingEffect.cs isn't used:

  - This was added for debugging but was never removed. We'll get rid of it to reduce maintenance.

- Empty TabbedPageRenderer.cs for Android:

  - This class is unnecessary, so we'll remove it.

- Rg.Plugin library is a leftover dependency:

  - This can also be removed, as it's no longer being used.

Before making any changes, commit the current state of the app to ensure we can revert if needed.

Removing Newtonsoft

Newtonsoft is currently used in the FitnessApiService in the FetchFromApiAsync method:

```
var content = await response.Content.ReadAsStringAsync();
var data = JsonConvert.DeserializeObject<T>(content);
return new Result<T>(data);
```

We can modify this in three simple steps:

1. Add the NuGet package System.Text.Json and remove Newtonsoft from the project. This is necessary because we are still using .NET Standard 2.0, which doesn't have System.Text.Json built-in. If you upgrade to a later .NET version, System.Text. Json comes by default.

2. Update the code to use System.Text.Json:

```
var content = await response.Content.
ReadAsStringAsync();
var data = System.Text.Json.JsonSerializer.
Deserialize<T>(content);
return new Result<T>(data);
```

3. Run and test the app, then commit the changes and push them to a separate branch (e.g., migration branch).

When migrating from Newtonsoft.Json to System.Text.Json, there are notable differences in functionality which you should be aware of.

For example, System.Text.Json lacks support for some features available in Newtonsoft.Json Many of these are not supported by design. For example:

1. System.Text.Json requires property names to be in quotes and does not support single quotes around string values.

2. Non-string JSON values can't be deserialized into string properties.

3. Advanced settings like TypeNameHandling.All for handling polymorphic types are not supported.

4. JsonPath queries, which allow complex filtering and selection within JSON data, are also unsupported.

5. System.Text.Json has limited configurability for handling large payloads, which may lead to restrictions for applications needing custom memory limits.

Also worth noting, by default, System.Text.Json uses case-sensitive property name matching during deserialization, which can lead to issues if your JSON and object property names don't match in case. To enable case-insensitive property matching, you can set JsonSerializerOptions. PropertyNameCaseInsensitive to true.

For example:

```
var options = new JsonSerializerOptions
{
    PropertyNameCaseInsensitive = true
};
var data = JsonSerializer.Deserialize<YourObjectType>
(jsonString, options);
```

Directly replacing Newtonsoft.Json with System.Text.Json may not always be feasible without making code changes. Review the differences, and alternatives, here:

```
https://learn.microsoft.com/en-us/dotnet/standard/
serialization/system-text-json/migrate-from-newtonsoft
```

Removing SkiaSharp

SkiaSharp is used in the `CustomImageViewOutlineProvider` class, but we don't need advanced features or optimizations for our simple image resizing task. We can replace SkiaSharp with Xamarin.Android's built-in image resizing capabilities.

79

1. Remove the SkiaSharp NuGet package.

2. Update the image resizing code:

    Before (SkiaSharp):

    ```
    var size = new SKSizeI(imageView.Width,
    imageView.Height);
    using var skiaBitmap = bitmap.ToSKBitmap();
    using var resizedBitmap = skiaBitmap.Resize(size,
    SKFilterQuality.High);
    var scaledBitmap = resizedBitmap?.ToBitmap();
    ```

    After (Xamarin.Android API):

    ```
    var scaledBitmap = Bitmap.CreateScaledBitmap
    (bitmapDrawable.Bitmap,
        bitmapDrawable.Bitmap.Width,
        bitmapDrawable.Bitmap.Height,
        filter: true);
    ```

    This works only on Android, so it wouldn't function
    in the shared project or iOS.

3. Run and test the app again. Commit and push the changes.

Removing Empty or Unused Classes

We don't want to clutter our code with unused classes, and therefore we'll remove the following unused classes and dependencies:

- LoggingEffect.cs

- TabbedPageRenderer.cs

Additionally, we'll remove the Rg.Plugin library and its associated initialization code from SplashActivity.cs and AppDelegate:

```
Rg.Plugins.Popup.Popup.Init(this);
```

Make separate commits for each of these changes and push them to the remote repository.

Now that we've cleaned up unnecessary code and dependencies, we're ready to start the migration by using the .NET Upgrade Assistant. This tool will handle much of the heavy lifting by updating our project structure and converting key components to their .NET MAUI equivalents.

Let's proceed!

.NET Upgrade Assistant

The .NET Upgrade Assistant helps simplify the process of migrating Xamarin.Forms projects to .NET MAUI by automating many key tasks that are typically error-prone or tedious. Here's what it does:

- Converts Xamarin.Forms, Xamarin.iOS, and Xamarin. Android projects to the SDK-style format.

- Updates the target framework to net8.0-android and net8.0-ios.

- Adds the <UseMaui>true</UseMaui> property in project files.

- Adds necessary project properties while removing outdated ones.

- Manages NuGet packages, removing Xamarin. Essentials (which is now a part of .NET MAUI). The Xamarin.CommunityToolkit package is replaced with the .NET MAUI Community Toolkit. Xamarin. Forms is removed; namespaces are replaced with the new Microsoft.Maui and Microsoft.Maui.Controls namespaces.

Although the migration process is made much simpler by the tool, there are still some manual tasks involved, particularly when working with custom renderers, platform-specific code, and complex UI layouts. For this reason, even if you use the Upgrade Assistant, you'll still need to go through the code to resolve certain cases, especially when refactoring legacy patterns to modern .NET MAUI equivalents.

Visual Studio Extension vs. CLI Tool

While the .NET Upgrade Assistant can be used as a command-line tool on macOS, the Visual Studio extension offers a user-friendly interface for those who prefer a visual approach. The CLI tool however works on Windows as well as MacOS, and we'll use the CLI tool, so we won't have to switch environments.

Installing the .NET Upgrade Assistant in Visual Studio

You can install the .NET Upgrade Assistant through Visual Studio's Extension Manager:

- In the main menu, select Extensions ➤ Manage Extensions.

- Search for Upgrade Assistant.

- Install the extension and restart Visual Studio.

Installing the .NET Upgrade Assistant CLI Tool

Assuming you already have dotnet installed, you can simply run the following in your preferred command line which will install it globally:

```
dotnet tool install -g upgrade-assistant
```

Once installed, the Upgrade Assistant can guide you through much of the migration process, leaving you with fewer manual changes to handle. However, you'll still need to review your project for more complex cases, such as third-party library compatibility and custom platform code. This is particularly important for projects that use Xamarin-specific features, custom renderers, or platform effects.

Migrating Project Structure, Namespaces, and Dependencies

In this section, we'll use the tool to migrate the main project. I'll cover the steps for the CLI tool as they do the same things behind the scenes. The fundamental difference is that the extension visualizes the steps and the results, but the steps, information, and output are the same. The extension equivalent of the CLI tool upgrade command is to right-click a project and select Upgrade from the context menu (Figure 6-1).

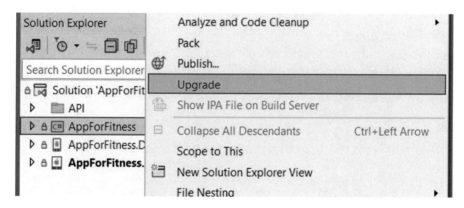

Figure 6-1. *The Update Assistant adds an Upgrade option to the project context menu in Visual Studio*

As for the CLI tool, which will be our preferred method in this book, we'll simply use our favorite terminal or command-line tool, navigate to the solution root, and run

```
upgrade-assistant upgrade
```

The tool is going to the projects it finds:

```
Which project do you want to upgrade (found 3)?

> AppForFitness (AppForFitness/AppForFitness.csproj)
  AppForFitness.Droid (AppForFitness.Droid/AppForFitness.
  Droid.csproj)
  AppForFitness.iOS (AppForFitness.iOS/AppForFitness.
  iOS.csproj)

  Navigation
    Exit
```

We have three projects, and we want to select the shared project, not the platform-specific projects. If your solution has additional non-platform-specific projects with Xamarin.Forms dependencies, run the tool for those as well when you have followed the steps for the shared project.

The tool will always give the option to continue, or exit, so I'll omit these lines from here on. The extension tool in Visual Studio has the same steps and options:

```
How do you want to upgrade project AppForFitness?

  In-place project upgrade (framework.inplace)
> Side-by-side project upgrade (framework.sidebyside)
```

In-place: This option upgrades your project without making a copy.

Side-by-side: This option copies your project and upgrades the copy, leaving the original project alone.

Let's discuss the options in more detail.

In-Place vs. Side-by-Side Migration

The choice depends on your project's complexity, the risk tolerance for disruption, and whether you want to keep your original Xamarin.Forms project intact.

In-Place Migration

What it does: This option upgrades your project directly without creating a copy.

When to choose it:

- If you're confident in your migration plan and want to minimize duplication.

- Your project has been fully backed up via version control or manual means.

- You prefer to directly modify the current project files and don't foresee needing to refer to the original Xamarin.Forms setup.

- You're working with a simple or smaller project with fewer dependencies and platform-specific code.

Side-by-Side Migration

What it does: This creates a copy of your project and upgrades the copy, leaving the original project intact.

When to choose it:

- If you want to keep the original Xamarin.Forms project unchanged, allowing you to maintain it while you experiment or slowly transition parts of the app to .NET MAUI.

- Your project is large and complex, with numerous platform-specific dependencies, and you need to do careful testing or incremental migration.

- If you're unsure whether the migration will go smoothly and want to compare the two projects during the transition.

- You want the flexibility to continue working on the Xamarin.Forms version while migrating certain platforms or features first in the new MAUI setup.

AppForFitness Side-by-Side Migration

Let's disregard the fact that AppForFitness is a simple app and imagine it as something more sophisticated. Also, we might want to refer to the Xamarin.Forms projects when we make changes, so we'll select side-by-side, create a new project, and call it AppForFitnessMaui. We can always do a name change when we are done.

In the next step, we can select the Target Framework, and we'll go with the option of the latest Long-Term Support (LTS) version of .NET, which at the time of writing is .NET 8.

When the tool finishes, it outputs the result:

```
Complete: 27 succeeded, 0 failed, 16 skipped.
```

If you want to skip the step by step, you can use the following line:

```
upgrade-assistant upgrade <PROJECT_PATH> --operation
    SideBySide --targetFramework LTS
--destination <NEW_PROJECT_NAME_OR_PATH>
```

You'll see the details of the migration if you scroll up, although they might not be so easy to read. Copy the terminal output to a file for a better overview. In Visual Studio, the Upgrade Assistant Window will show the results using icons for the result.

For example, for this app, most of our items have a green checkmark, but a couple have a lighter shade. These have the following message:

```
No applicable transformations found for this component, it
is left unchanged. See details in the Upgrade Assistant
output pane.
```

In Visual Studio, you can view the output in the Output window by using the drop-down to select Upgrade Assistant (Figure 6-2).

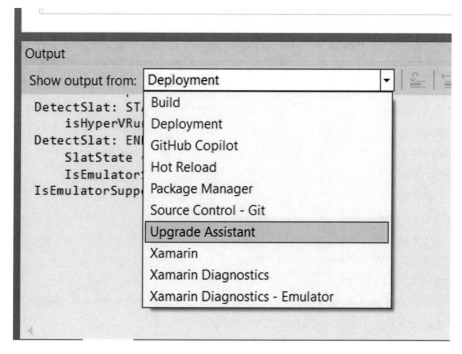

Figure 6-2. *While the CLI tool shows the output in the terminal, the extension in Visual Studio outputs the details in the Output window*

If you have several SDKs installed in your solution, and it causes build problems, I highly recommend adding a `global.json` file to the migrated shared project specifying the SDK version and roll forward policy and whether to allow prerelease versions:

```json
{
  "sdk": {
    "version": "8.0.0",
    "rollForward": "latestMajor",
    "allowPrerelease": false
  }
}
```

The migrated shared project is going to use the structure we had for our shared Xamarin.Forms project, with some additions such as new dependencies. But most noticeable is the MauiProgramExtensions.cs. This class extends the configuration of the MauiAppBuilder by introducing a custom extension method, UseSharedMauiApp. This method allows us to configure our app and platform logic and is called as part of the app's startup pipeline. When you create a brand-new Single Project .NET MAUI project, you'll get a MainProgram.cs instead, which essentially does the same thing.

We'll cover the structure of a .NET MAUI project later in this chapter when we create our main .NET MAUI project, where we'll move all the code. As mentioned earlier, the migrated shared project is only temporary. Once we have addressed the errors and made it build, we will move the content to a new project.

But, before we do anything more, we'll commit the work in progress with an appropriate commit message, for example:

```
WIP Shared project to MAUI - not building
```

Updating Dependencies

Generally, I'd say that the best place to start after running the Upgrade Assistant is dealing with dependencies. Our inventory list is of great help, and we can use it to identify the dependencies that need an upgrade or replacement.

Based on the details from the Upgrade Assistant, AppForFitness doesn't have a lot of issues that need addressing, but there is one that we can address: the OxyPlot dependency. If we start a build, we'll also get an error:

```
This project or a dependency has imported the Xamarin.Forms
packages. .NET MAUI is not compatible with Xamarin.Forms and is
unable to build. Please remove Xamarin.Forms or the project/
package dependency that is using Xamarin.Forms.
```

In Explorer, there is even a warning triangle at the Dependency node. The Upgrade Assistant will not update all dependencies, so this is expected. A quick search in NuGet Explorer, and we can find a .NET MAUI alternative, which ironically depends on SkiaSharp (Figure 6-3). This means we'll indirectly bring back the SkiaSharp dependency. But that's okay, as mentioned earlier, SkiaSharp is a mature open source project.

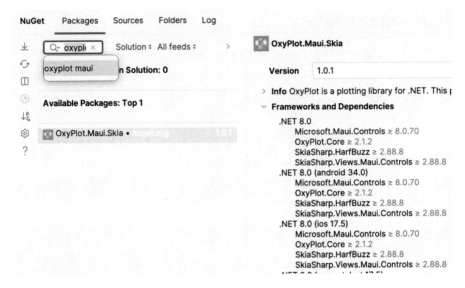

Figure 6-3. *OxyPlot has a version that supports .NET MAUI*

With the replacement in place, the error list grows considerably in the Problems window (Error window in Visual Studio). We might as well continue solving the errors related to the OxyPlot package so the next commit can be somewhat scoped.

These are the errors I fixed in the OxyPlot commit.

The ToOxyColor extension method is missing, so I went ahead and created one in a ColorExtensions class:

```
public static class ColorExtensions {
    public static OxyColor ToOxyColor(this Color
    mauiColor) {
        return OxyColor.FromArgb((byte)(mauiColor.
        Alpha * 255),
                                (byte)(mauiColor.
                                Red * 255),
                                (byte)(mauiColor.
                                Green * 255),
```

```
(byte)(mauiColor.Blue
* 255));
        }
    }
```

I also update the namespace references for OxyPlot, on the XAML.cs file, as well as the XAML file:

```
xmlns:oxyPlot="clr-namespace:OxyPlot.Maui.
Skia;assembly=OxyPlot.Maui.Skia"
```

Updating Namespaces

You've probably noticed by now that the Upgrade Assistant didn't change the namespaces to match the new project name. Since this is an intermediary project, we don't really need to update the namespaces as we'll have to update them again once we move the code. Renaming the namespaces is an easy fix as both Rider and Visual Studio has quick actions for this (Figure 6-4). If you use an IDE that doesn't support this, then a Find and Replace can do the trick as well.

Figure 6-4. *Both Rider and Visual Studio have quick actions to do refactoring, such as renaming namespaces*

Quick actions are nice, but won't cover all the references that need renaming. For example, in XAML files if you've referenced the project assembly, you'll have problems as the assembly has a new name. Find this:

```
assembly=AppForFitness"
```

And replace with this:

```
assembly=AppForFitnessMaui"
```

We aren't done with namespaces and references. If you take a look at the errors in the Problems window (Error window in Visual Studio), you'll probably see a few with this error code: CS01104.

```
X is ambiguous reference between Y and Z
```

This error is commonly seen where the Compatibility package is referenced. The MAUI compatibility package lets you transition easier to MAUI, but it also comes at a cost. Some of the most challenging bugs we encountered were directly related to the compatibility package, leading me to recommend avoiding it whenever possible. For example, for Grid, use the MAUI grid, not the compatibility grid.

Being this early in the migration process, I recommend you remove the reference to the Compatibility package where there is a direct equivalent in .NET MAUI. By this point, we know the Grid is very different, in particular because the rows and columns have to be explicitly added. And we know *AndExpand is not supported, but we'll ignore all that for now, to get to a build.

In the files where you don't want to remove the Compatibility package, say, for example, StackLayout, you can add an aliased reference. Right-click the type and select the reference, and Rider or Visual Studio will add one for you. Do not do this for all in one go; you really want to do this one reference at a time:

```
using StackLayout = Microsoft.Maui.Controls.Compatibility.
StackLayout;
```

Note that properties that are tied to a specific compatibility control, for example, RelativeLayout.XConstraint, will also need a reference:

```
<StackLayout Padding="10">
        <Frame HasShadow="False">
                <Frame.Effects>
                        <effects:ShadowEffect />
                </Frame.Effects>
                <StackLayout>
        <compatibility:RelativeLayout Padding="10"
VerticalOptions="Start">
        <customControls:IconButton x:Name="image"
                                        Clicked="OnIconClicked"
                                        Source="dumbells.png"
                                        HeightRequest="70"
                                        WidthRequest="70"
                                        compatibility:RelativeLayout.
                                        YConstraint="{compatibility:
                                        ConstraintExpression
                                        Type=Constant, Constant=10}"
                                        compatibility:RelativeLayout.
                                        XConstraint="{compatibility:
                                        ConstraintExpression
                                        Type=Constant,
                                        Constant=10}"/>
```

Here is a list of other namespace changes:

Xamarin.Forms Namespace	.NET MAUI Namespace(s)
Xamarin.Forms	Microsoft.Maui and Microsoft.Maui.Controls
Xamarin.Forms.DualScreen	Microsoft.Maui.Controls.Foldable
Xamarin.Forms.Maps	Microsoft.Maui.Controls.Maps and Microsoft.Maui.Maps
Xamarin.Forms.PlatformConfiguration	Microsoft.Maui.Controls.PlatformConfiguration
Xamarin.Forms.PlatformConfiguration.AndroidSpecific	Microsoft.Maui.Controls.PlatformConfiguration.AndroidSpecific
Xamarin.Forms.PlatformConfiguration.AndroidSpecific.AppCompat	Microsoft.Maui.Controls.PlatformConfiguration.AndroidSpecific.AppCompat
Xamarin.Forms.PlatformConfiguration.TizenSpecific	Microsoft.Maui.Controls.PlatformConfiguration.TizenSpecific
Xamarin.Forms.PlatformConfiguration.WindowsSpecific	Microsoft.Maui.Controls.PlatformConfiguration.WindowsSpecific
Xamarin.Forms.PlatformConfiguration.iOSSpecific	Microsoft.Maui.Controls.PlatformConfiguration.iOSSpecific
Xamarin.Forms.Shapes	Microsoft.Maui.Controls.Shapes
Xamarin.Forms.StyleSheets	Microsoft.Maui.Controls.StyleSheets
Xamarin.Forms.Xaml	Microsoft.Maui.Controls.Xaml

Sort out the error in this category one by one, commit, push, and try to build. If you encounter build errors that are not related to dependencies, code logic, references, namespaces, or alike, have a look at Appendix B.

Creating Our Main Project

At this point in the migration, we have migrated the shared project, but it won't be able to deploy to neither of our target platforms. The project is a temporary project, as we'll create a new .NET MAUI project where we'll move all our files. Why? A new MAUI project will give us the default folder structure and everything else we need to deploy to our target platforms, which will save us time. Create a new project using the .NET MAUI template (Figure 6-5).

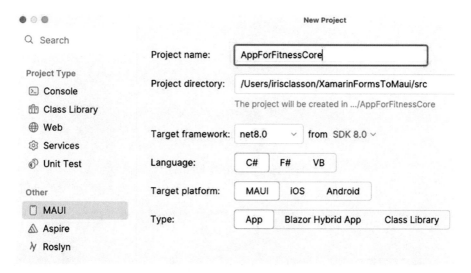

Figure 6-5. *Create a new .NET MAUI project*

The .NET project template has a predetermined structure. Here's a breakdown of the folders and their significance in the .NET MAUI default template (Figure 6-6).

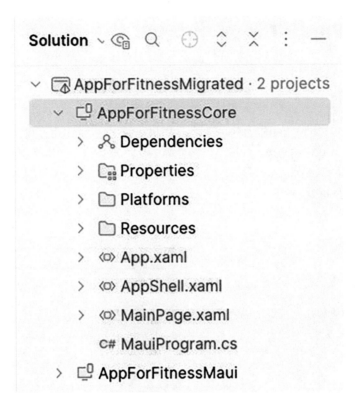

Figure 6-6. *.NET MAUI single project structure*

Dependencies

This section lists the NuGet packages and the SDK versions your project targets.

Platforms

These folders contain platform-specific code and resources. If you need to write code or include assets that are platform specific, you do that in these folders. This is the equivalent of our platform projects in Xamarin.Forms and where we'll move our files.

For example:

- In Android, you might have the AndroidManifest.xml and platform-specific resources.

- In iOS, you'll have iOS-specific files such as the Info.plist.

Resources

This is a shared resources folder that allows you to manage cross-platform resources centrally:

- AppIcon: This folder contains the icons for the app, and these icons are shared across all platforms.

- Fonts: You can place any custom fonts in this folder, and they will be available to all platforms.

- Images: This is where you put your shared images. MAUI will automatically handle loading the correct image size for each platform (e.g., retina images for iOS).

- Raw: A folder where raw files (like videos or other assets) can be placed and accessed by your app.

- Splash: Contains splash screen assets, which are used when the app is starting.

- Styles: This folder stores styles for your app that are shared across all platforms. In MAUI, resource dictionaries are used for things like colors, styles, and other theme-related configurations.

App.xaml/App.xaml.cs

This is the entry point for your application. It defines shared resources for your app and initializes the app's components. It is where global styles and resource dictionaries can be defined.

AppShell.xaml/AppShell.xaml.cs

.NET MAUI uses the Shell concept to simplify navigation in your app. The AppShell.xaml file contains your app's navigation structure (e.g., tabs, flyouts, routes), which can be customized to manage how users navigate between pages.

MainPage.xaml/MainPage.xaml.cs

This is the default starting page of the application. It is created by default when you create a new .NET MAUI project.

MauiProgram.cs

This file is the main configuration file for your app. It follows a similar pattern to ASP.NET Core's Startup.cs and is where services, configurations, fonts, handlers, and dependencies are registered using the MauiApp. CreateBuilder() method.

Cleaning Up the .NET MAUI Project

The default template targets additional platforms, so before we continue, we are going to clean up the new project. The additional target frameworks are reference in the project file under the target frameworks node. Remove additional targets and comments:

```
<PropertyGroup>
    <TargetFrameworks>net8.0-android;net8.0-ios;net8.0-
    maccatalyst</TargetFrameworks>
    <TargetFrameworks Condition="$([MSBuild]::IsOSPl
    atform('windows'))">$(TargetFrameworks);net8.0-
    windows10.0.19041.0</TargetFrameworks>
    <!-- Uncomment to also build the tizen app. You will
    need to install tizen by following this: https://
    github.com/Samsung/Tizen.NET -->
    <!-- <TargetFrameworks>$(TargetFrameworks);net8.0-
    tizen</TargetFrameworks> -->

    <!-- Note for MacCatalyst:
    The default runtime is maccatalyst-x64, except
    in Release config, in which case the default is
    maccatalyst-x64;maccatalyst-arm64.
    When specifying both architectures, use the plural
    <RuntimeIdentifiers> instead of the singular
    <RuntimeIdentifier>.
    The Mac App Store will NOT accept apps with ONLY
    maccatalyst-arm64 indicated;
    either BOTH runtimes must be indicated or ONLY
    macatalyst-x64. -->
    <!-- For example: <RuntimeIdentifiers>maccatalyst-
    x64;maccatalyst-arm64</RuntimeIdentifiers> -->
```

To this:

```
<PropertyGroup>
    <TargetFrameworks>net8.0-android;net8.0-ios;</
    TargetFrameworks>
    <OutputType>Exe</OutputType>
```

Also, remove the folders for the targets that were removed. If on Windows, make sure the folder was in fact deleted by double-checking in File Explorer or using the command line.

Build the new project, verifying everything works.

Commit and push to remote source control.

Merging the Migrated Project and .NET MAUI Project

Merging the two is straightforward and requires very little work. These are the steps:

Step 1: Delete files we already have.

In the .NET MAUI project, delete the following files as we already have these in the migrated shared project:

- App.XAML and cs file

- AppShell.XAML and cs file

- MainPage.XAML and cs file

Step 2: Copy over references.

We want to make sure we have the dependencies in the new project, so open the project file for the migrated shared project, and copy the references:

```
<PackageReference Include="OxyPlot.Maui.Skia"
Version="1.0.1" />
```

Paste these in the AppForFitnessMigrated project file:

```
<ItemGroup>
    <PackageReference Include="Microsoft.Maui.Controls"
    Version="$(MauiVersion)" />
    <PackageReference Include="Microsoft.Maui.Controls.
    Compatibility" Version="$(MauiVersion)" />
```

```
    <PackageReference Include="Microsoft.Extensions.
    Logging.Debug" Version="8.0.0" />
  <PackageReference Include="OxyPlot.Maui.Skia"
  Version="1.0.1" />
  </ItemGroup>
```

Step 3: Drag in the files from the migrated shared project to the .NET MAUI project. Update namespaces; clean up MainProgram.cs if needed. Commit and push.

Test Deploying

If we try to deploy the app now, we'll encounter an error because we haven't added .UseMauiCompatibility() to the MauiProgram.cs file. This method is essential for maintaining backward compatibility with Xamarin. Forms components that haven't yet been updated to work with native .NET MAUI code.

To fix this issue, you'll need to modify your MauiProgram.cs file. Here's how you add .UseMauiCompatibility() to the builder pattern:

```
public static class MauiProgram
{
    public static MauiApp CreateMauiApp()
    {
        var builder = MauiApp.CreateBuilder();
        builder
            .UseMauiApp<App>()
            .UseMauiCompatibility()  // Add this line
            .ConfigureFonts(fonts =>
            {
                fonts.AddFont("OpenSans-Regular.ttf",
                "OpenSansRegular");
```

```
            fonts.AddFont("OpenSans-Semibold.ttf",
            "OpenSansSemibold");
    });

    return builder.Build();
  }
}
```

Don't forget to add a reference:

```
using Microsoft.Maui.Controls.Compatibility.Hosting;
```

The Builder Pattern in .NET MAUI

As mentioned earlier, the builder pattern is a popular design pattern used across various .NET frameworks, including .NET MAUI. The essence of the builder pattern is to construct complex objects step by step. In the context of .NET MAUI, this means you use the MauiApp.CreateBuilder() to configure services, dependencies, and platform-specific resources in a fluent, chainable manner.

Here's how the builder pattern is used in .NET MAUI.

Step-by-step initialization: The builder pattern allows developers to initialize and configure services, middleware, and platform-specific properties in a clear and structured way. This enables a step-by-step approach to app configuration.

For example:

```
builder.ConfigureFonts(fonts =>
{
    fonts.AddFont("OpenSans-Regular.ttf", "OpenSansRegular");
});
```

Chaining configurations: It's possible to chain multiple configurations together. For example, we configure fonts, handlers, services, and other platform-specific settings in one smooth chain.

Cross-platform consistency: The builder pattern ensures that configuration remains consistent across different platforms. It centralizes the app's setup logic in one place, reducing duplication and platform-specific discrepancies.

If we try to run the app again, we get another error indicating that we are missing another chain configuration. The error itself is as follows:

```
Handler not found for view SkiaSharp.Views.Maui.Controls.
SKCanvasView.
```

We haven't talked much about handlers, but in this particular case, it's not one of our own handlers missing. I took a look at the OxyPlotMaui sample app and noticed that they register OxyPlot using chain configuration in the builder. This code essentially replaces the init code we removed when we updated the package to the .NET MAUI version.

This is how it's registered now:

```
builder
    .UseMauiApp<App>()
    .UseMauiCompatibility()
    // Add these two:
    .UseSkiaSharp()
    .UseOxyPlotSkia()
    .ConfigureFonts(fonts => {
        fonts.AddFont("OpenSans-Regular.ttf",
        "OpenSansRegular");
        fonts.AddFont("OpenSans-Semibold.ttf",
        "OpenSansSemibold");
    });
```

As you can see, even without the platform-specific code we can get somewhat up and running.

You could be lucky and be able to deploy the app to a simulator, emulator, or device without errors. It won't look pretty, as not only do the UI layout and controls differ, we are also missing our platform-specific implementations. However, try to deploy on the target platforms and assess the result before we move on to the next step, migrating the platform-specific projects.

Dependency Injection in .NET MAUI

In .NET MAUI, dependency injection (DI) is built-in, making it easier to handle dependencies without relying on DependencyService as used in Xamarin.Forms. This allows you to inject services directly into pages, services, or view models without needing manual lookups.

Replacing Xamarin.Forms DependencyService with .NET MAUI DI

In Xamarin.Forms, services were typically registered like this:

```
[assembly: Dependency(typeof(SecureStorageService_iOS))]
```

Then retrieved like this:

```
var storageService = DependencyService.
Get<ISecureStorageService>();
```

In .NET MAUI, you now leverage the built-in DI container to register and use services.

Step 1: Register the Service in MauiProgram.cs

Within MauiProgram.cs, services are registered using the builder pattern. For example, to register ISecureStorageService, you'd do this:

```
public static class MauiProgram
{
    public static MauiApp CreateMauiApp()
```

```
{
    var builder = MauiApp.CreateBuilder();
    builder
        .UseMauiApp<App>()
        .ConfigureFonts(fonts =>
        {
            fonts.AddFont("OpenSans-Regular.ttf",
            "OpenSansRegular");
        });

    // Register your services here
    builder.Services.AddSingleton<ISecureStorageService,
    TmpSecureStorage>();

    return builder.Build();
    }
}
```

Step 2: Create a Temporary Implementation

To keep the momentum during migration, we can implement a dummy version of the service with a TODO comment reminding us to complete it later. Here's an example of a temporary implementation for the secure storage service:

```
//TODO: Implement the real secure storage service later
public class TmpSecureStorage : ISecureStorageService
{
    public Task StoreDataAsync(string key, string value) =>
    Task.CompletedTask;

    public Task<string> GetDataAsync(string key) => Task.
    FromResult("something");
}
```

Step 3: Injecting the Service in a Page

Once the service is registered, inject it into the constructor of any class (like a page or view model) that needs it. Here's how you inject it into ProgressPage.cs:

```
public class ProgressPage : ContentPage
{
    private readonly ISecureStorageService _storageService;

    public ProgressPage(ISecureStorageService storageService)
    {
        _storageService = storageService;
        InitializeComponent();
    }

    // Use the injected service
    public async Task LoadUserData()
    {
        var userId = await _storageService.GetDataAsync
        (Config.UserId);
        // Use the retrieved data
    }
}
```

Use constructor injection where the storage service is needed.

DI gives us compile-time safety as services are registered and injected with compile-time checks, making the app more reliable. We can easily manage service lifetimes (e.g., Singleton, Scoped) with .NET MAUI's DI, and it reduces coupling and makes it easier to test and maintain code.

A Quick Mention: Navigation

When we build again, we meet our next challenge: navigation.

Our EntryPage has the following code:

```
private async void OnSaveEntryClicked(object sender,
EventArgs e) {
    var exercises = (await ExerciseCatalogueCacheService.
    Instance.GetExercisesCatalogueAsync()).Exercises;
    var id = exercises.First(x => x.Name == _
    preSelectedExerciseName).Id;
    var newLift = new Lift(_selectedReps, _selectedWeight,
    DateTime.Now, Guid.NewGuid(), id);
    await _apiService.SaveExerciseEntryAsync(_selectedExercise,
    newLift);
    saveEntryBtn.IsEnabled = false;
    if (Navigation.NavigationStack.Any()) {
        await Navigation.PopAsync();
    } else {
        await Navigation.PushAsync(new ProgressPage());
    }
}
```

This won't work now that we inject ISecureStorageService in the constructor. In .NET MAUI, navigation works similarly to Xamarin.Forms, but it is streamlined with Shell navigation and improvements in page navigation.

We will talk more about Navigation in the next chapter. But even with this fix, this won't quite solve our issues. MainPage directly uses the ProgressPage in its XAML view, and ProgressPage doesn't have a default constructor.

We don't have this issue in App.cs as the builder creates it, and it knows to inject the dependency. ProgressPage tabbed item is different though.

If we comment out the ProgressPage in MainPage, the app launches:

```
<TabbedPage.Children>
    <!-- TODO add back -->
    <!-- <views:ProgressPage Title="Progress"/> -->
    <views:EntryPage Title="New Entry"/>
    <views:SettingsPage Title="Settings"/>
</TabbedPage.Children>
```

Dependency injection does always jell well with code-behind, mostly because code-behind isn't as flexible, and thus testable and maintainable, as DI. In an ideal world, we'd refactor our app to be more flexible with bindings and view models, but that would be outside of the scope of this book.

IServiceProvider

To make MainPage work without rewriting too much of our logic, we could, for example, inject the IServiceProvider. The IServiceProvider is a core interface in .NET's dependency injection (DI) system and can be used to retrieve services from the DI container. If we register the ProgressPage in the builder, we can do something like this:

```
public MainPage(IServiceProvider _serviceProvider) {
    InitializeComponent();
    _popupService = new PopupService();
    Children.Insert(0, (Page)_serviceProvider.GetService
    (typeof(ProgressPage)));
}
```

Handler.MauiContext.Services

Another option is to use the OnHandlerChanged method which exists in the base class and can be overridden. This is a part of the page lifecycle, which we'll cover soon.

Inside it, we can check if the Handler for the class is available, with its MauiContext, and if so access the DI container and retrieve an instance of ISecureStorageService.

This approach is used to safely access services in MAUI when you don't have direct access to the dependency injection container through constructor injection. It's a way to bridge the gap between MAUI's UI lifecycle and the application's service container; however, as mentioned earlier, while this method works, it's generally preferable to use constructor injection when possible, as it makes dependencies more explicit and easier to manage and test, but then the rest of the class has to follow suit.

With the constructor injection removed, I set the storage service like this instead:

```
protected override void OnHandlerChanged()
{
    base.OnHandlerChanged();

    if (Handler is not null && _storageService is null)
    {
        _storageService = Handler.MauiContext?.Services.GetServ
        ice<ISecureStorageService>();
    }
}
```

It's not as clean or explicit as constructor injection and can make dependencies less obvious to other developers reading the code. In addition, it might lead to null reference exceptions if the service is used before OnHandlerChanged is called, and it mixes concerns of UI and service initialization.

While this works, and our app builds, we will get back to this when we discuss navigation in the next chapter. But for now, let's commit and push, happy that we have a working app (albeit without platform-specific code).

Summary

In this chapter, we took our first big steps in migrating the AppForFitness solution from Xamarin.Forms to .NET MAUI. We started with important cleanup tasks, including removing unused dependencies like Newtonsoft and SkiaSharp, simplifying the codebase in preparation for migration.

We used the .NET Upgrade Assistant to automate some aspects of the migration, converting project structures and updating key components. The focus was on upgrading the shared project, creating a new .NET MAUI project and moving the files. As we have dealt with errors and configurations, we've learned more about some of the default design patterns in .NET MAUI, and we will cover more of that as we migrate.

In the next chapter, we will dive deeper into platform-specific migration and UI differences and more.

CHAPTER 7

Migrating Platform Projects

With the shared project successfully migrated, it's time to focus on the platform-specific projects (iOS and Android). While the app may now build, it's still far from fully functional. For many projects, particularly more complex ones, the app may not even build at this stage. You may encounter issues because some platform-specific code hasn't yet been migrated. For instance, we created a temporary dummy implementation for our storage service earlier, but if your app contains many such services, it could become a tedious and complex task.

Dummy Classes and Mocks

One way to simplify migration, especially if there's a lot of missing platform-specific functionality, is to use a mocking library. A mocking library can dynamically create mocks for your dependencies and class members, which can be useful in filling the gaps for services you haven't yet migrated. However, it's important to note that this approach, while useful in testing environments, is not recommended for production code. If your code isn't loosely coupled or highly modular, using a mocking library could be more trouble than it's worth.

© Iris Classon 2025
I. Classon, *Migrating from Xamarin.Forms to .NET MAUI*,
https://doi.org/10.1007/979-8-8688-1215-6_7

Ultimately, the best approach is to migrate platform-specific code as early as possible in the migration process. Let's start by moving the platform-specific code for iOS.

Migrating the iOS Platform Project

The first step is to copy over the platform code from the original Xamarin. Forms iOS project to the Platforms/iOS folder in your new .NET MAUI project. Be selective here—exclude files like Main.cs and AppDelegate.cs, as these will be handled differently in .NET MAUI.

In the AppForFitness project, for example, the Main.cs file is primarily used to register OxyPlot, which has already been handled with a handler extension in our .NET MAUI code. If your iOS platform project contains more complex logic, you'll need to move it manually, placing initialization logic in either Program.cs (inside the Platforms/iOS folder) or the MauiProgram.cs file.

AppDelegate

In AppDelegate, we had some deep linking logic to navigate to specific pages when the app is opened through a URL. We'll need to migrate this logic to the new AppDelegate.cs in .NET MAUI. Here's how you can update it:

```
using AppForFitnessCore.Services;
using Foundation;
using UIKit;
```

```
namespace AppForFitnessCore
{
    [Register("AppDelegate")]
    public class AppDelegate : MauiUIApplicationDelegate
    {
        protected override MauiApp CreateMauiApp() =>
        MauiProgram.CreateMauiApp();

        public override bool OpenUrl(UIApplication app,
        NSUrl url, NSDictionary options)
        {
            if (url.AbsoluteString == null) return false;
            var uri = new Uri(url.AbsoluteString);
            DeepLinkingService.HandleDeepLink(uri);
            return true;
        }
    }
}
```

This code ensures that the app can still handle deep linking on iOS as it did in Xamarin.Forms. We'll deal with navigation and deep linking further in the navigation section of this book.

Namespace Renaming and Cleanup

After moving the files to the Platforms/iOS folder, you should rename any namespaces to reflect their new location. Following that, here are some additional cleanup tasks you'll want to do for the AppForFitness project:

1. Remove ColorExtensions.cs: This class has been re-implemented in the .NET MAUI project, so there's no need for the old version.

2.   Remove Xamarin.Forms references: Make sure all remaining Xamarin.Forms references are removed from the platform-specific files.

3.   Remove DependencyService usage: If you're still using the old [assembly: Dependency] attributes (e.g., [assembly: Dependency(typeof(SecureStorag eService_iOS))]), remove these, as .NET MAUI now uses dependency injection (DI).

4.   Rename {X}Renderer to {X}Handler: In Xamarin. Forms, platform-specific UI changes were handled by renderers. In .NET MAUI, these are replaced by Handlers. Go through the code and rename any instances of {X}Renderer to {X}Handler. You can use a regular expression (regex) in a Find and Replace to quickly do this (Figure 7-1):

Find: `public\s+class\s+(\w+)Renderer`
Replace: `public class $1Handler`

Figure 7-1. *Regex search and replace in Rider is powerful. If you want more control over the results, try narrowing down the search to a specific directory*

5. Remove the assembly attribute for renderers; we won't need them.

Understanding Handlers in .NET MAUI

In .NET MAUI, the Handler pattern replaces the older renderer pattern from Xamarin.Forms. This shift is one of the most significant changes in the way platform-specific customization is handled in .NET MAUI. Understanding how handlers work will help us customize controls across different platforms more efficiently, with better performance and less code.

What Are Handlers?

Handlers act as a bridge between cross-platform code and platform-specific implementations in .NET MAUI. Unlike renderers, which involve creating a completely new platform-specific subclass for each control, handlers provide a lightweight, performance-focused way to interact with native controls.

Each handler in .NET MAUI is responsible for

- Mapping the properties of a cross-platform control to the corresponding native control on each platform

- Managing the lifecycle of the native control

In simpler terms, handlers remove the need to deal with platform-specific intricacies by offering a unified API for the shared project. This makes cross-platform development faster, with fewer performance issues and maintenance overhead.

Key Differences from Renderers

- Performance: Handlers are generally faster than renderers, as they are more efficient in how they handle platform-specific elements.

- Customizability: Handlers allow developers to easily customize platform-specific behavior without the need for overriding or subclassing controls.

- Flexible mappings: With handlers, properties are mapped more flexibly between cross-platform controls and their native counterparts, avoiding the tight coupling of renderers.

Let's use the IconButtonHandler (former IconButtonRenderer) as an example.

This is our old implementation:

```
public class IconButtonRenderer: ImageRenderer
{
    /// <summary>
    /// Called when the associated Xamarin.Forms element
        changes.
    /// </summary>
    /// <param name="e">Event arguments for the change.</param>
    protected override void OnElementChanged(ElementChangedEven
    tArgs<Image> e)
    {
        base.OnElementChanged(e);

        if (Control == null)
            return;

        if (e.NewElement is IconButton)
        {
            SetDropShadow();
        }
    }
}
```

Refactored version:

```
public class IconButtonHandler : ImageHandler
{
    protected override void ConnectHandler(UIImageView
    platformView)
    {
        base.ConnectHandler(platformView);

        // Add drop shadow to the platform-specific control
            (UIImageView)
        SetDropShadow(platformView);
    }

    private void SetDropShadow(UIImageView imageView)
    {
        imageView.Layer.ShadowOffset = new CGSize(0, 3);
        imageView.Layer.ShadowOpacity = 0.25f;
        imageView.Layer.ShadowRadius = 2.0f;
        imageView.ClipsToBounds = false;
    }

    protected override void DisconnectHandler(UIImageView
    platformView)
    {
        base.DisconnectHandler(platformView);
        // Any cleanup code can go here if needed
    }
}
```

As we begin extending the ImageHandler class, IntelliSense (Rider autocomplete) suggests the handlers shown in Figure 7-2. There are several handlers, and one of them is an ImageButtonHandler. There is also an Image Button that we could use instead, as well as a simpler way to deal with the drop shadow now that we've migrated to .NET MAUI, but we'll leave that for later.

```
/// <summary>
/// Custom renderer for the IconButton control in iOS to add drop shadows.
/// </summary>
  Iris Classon
public class IconButtonHandler : ImageHan
{
                              ImageHandler (in Microsoft.Maui.Handlers)
    /// <summary>
    /// Called when the assoc      ImageButtonHandler (in Microsoft.Maui.Handlers)
    /// </summary>                 IImageButtonHandler (in Microsoft.Maui.Handlers)
```

Figure 7-2. *The suggestions in the drop-down indicate there is an*
ImageButtonHandler, which means there is an ImageButton we could
use instead, but we'll take a look at that later in the book

Registering the Handler

Like we did with the OxyPlot handler, which was added as an extension
method, we'll register the handlers in the builder. However, to avoid
cluttering the entry point of the application with conditional compilation,
we'll instead use a delegate so we can register platform handlers in the
platform-specific entry points.

First, we have to change the CreateMauiApp signature:

```
public static MauiApp CreateMauiApp(Action<IMauiHandlersCollect
ion> handlerDelegate)
{
    var builder = MauiApp.CreateBuilder();
    builder
        .UseMauiApp<App>()
        .UseMauiCompatibility()
        .UseSkiaSharp()
        .UseOxyPlotSkia()
        .ConfigureMauiHandlers(handlerDelegate)
```

And then we can update our AppDelegate like this:

```
protected override MauiApp CreateMauiApp() => MauiProgram.
CreateMauiApp(handlerCollection =>
{
    handlerCollection
        .AddHandler(typeof(Image), typeof(IconButtonHandler));
});
```

The AddHandler method is a part of .NET MAUI and how we register handlers. It has two parameters, the view type and the handler type.

We'll have to change MainApplication.cs in the Android folder as well, even though we haven't moved over any code yet.

```
protected override MauiApp CreateMauiApp() => MauiProgram.
CreateMauiApp(handlerCollection =>
{
});
```

Let's talk about handler lifecycles.

Handler Lifecycle

In .NET MAUI, the handler lifecycle revolves around various events and methods that manage the creation, connection, and disconnection of platform-specific native controls with the cross-platform UI elements. Here's an overview of two main lifecycle events all handlers have:

- ConnectHandler

  - This method is invoked when the handler is connected to its platform view (i.e., when the cross-platform control is rendered into a platform-specific view).

- This is where you apply the initial setup, bindings, and any customization needed for the platform control.

- DisconnectHandler

  - This method is invoked when the handler is disconnected from the platform view (i.e., when the view is about to be destroyed or recycled).

  - You can use this method to clean up any resources or remove event listeners to avoid memory leaks.

Migrating the Other Renderers

We have two more renderers to deal with: the TabbedPageRenderer and the LongPressViewRenderer.

We'll keep this section short and summarize the migration, but you can look at the code for more details.

TabbedPageRenderer

The TabbedPageRenderer.cs was used to force iOS to use custom styling for the tabs. Since we aren't sure if we need this anymore, we'll just comment out the handler instead of migrating it and leave a //TODO comment so we don't forget about it.

LongPressViewRenderer

We migrated this renderer to a handler that extends the ContentViewHandler. Initially, I used the ViewHandler by mistake. However, since the custom control LongPressView inherits from ContentView, it made more sense to extend the ContentViewHandler to ensure we are matching the handler to the control's hierarchy.

Mappers vs. Handlers

Before we dive into more handler examples, it's worth noting that handlers aren't always needed. In some cases, it's better to modify or extend the behavior of existing controls using mappers.

What Are Mappers?

Mappers in .NET MAUI allow you to modify or append functionality to an existing handler, extending the control's behavior without completely overriding the platform-specific handler. Mappers are a cleaner, more modular way to apply platform-specific customizations while preserving existing logic and behavior.

Example of How Mappers Work

A mapper allows you to extend the platform-specific behavior of controls by mapping properties or methods of your control to the corresponding platform functionality. Here's how it works:

- Platform-specific logic: Each control in .NET MAUI has a base handler (e.g., ButtonHandler for buttons, ImageHandler for images). The handler takes care of platform-specific logic like rendering the control.

- Mapper: The mapper is where you can append to or modify the behavior of the handler. Instead of creating a custom handler from scratch, you can use a mapper to add custom behavior to the existing control.

Example: IconButtonMapper

To demonstrate, let's use the IconButton, a control we've referred to earlier, where shadows were added via a custom handler. Using mappers, we can achieve the same functionality with less code.

Here's how to add shadow functionality to IconButton by appending to the existing ImageHandler using a mapper:

```
public static class IconButtonMapper
{
    public static void MapIconButton()
    {
        ImageHandler.Mapper.AppendToMapping(nameof(IconButton),
        (handler, view) =>
        {
            if (view is IconButton)
            {
                handler.PlatformView.Layer.ShadowOffset = new
                CoreGraphics.CGSize(0, 3);
                handler.PlatformView.Layer.ShadowOpacity
                = 0.25f;
                handler.PlatformView.Layer.ShadowRadius = 2.0f;
                handler.PlatformView.ClipsToBounds = false;
            }
        });
    }
}
```

Here, we're adding shadow to the IconButton by leveraging the ImageHandler's mapper, and this keeps the existing functionality of ImageHandler intact.

Registering the Mapper in MauiProgram.cs

After defining the mapper, it needs to be registered in the MauiProgram.cs:

```
protected override MauiApp CreateMauiApp() => MauiProgram.
CreateMauiApp(handlerCollection =>
{
```

```
handlerCollection
    .AddHandler(typeof(LongPressView),
    typeof(LongPressViewHandler));
IconButtonMapper.MapIconButton(); // Register the
IconButton mapper here
});
```

By appending behavior through mappers, you can extend platform-specific functionality without replacing or recreating handlers from scratch. Keep in mind that we've so far only implemented this for the iOS platform.

Here are some of the primary methods related to mappers.

AppendToMapping

This method is used to add additional behavior to an existing mapping without overriding it completely. You can append platform-specific behavior or cross-platform extensions:

```
ImageHandler.Mapper.AppendToMapping(nameof(IconButton),
(handler, view) =>
{
    // Add platform-specific logic for IconButton
});
```

ReplaceMapping

This method is used to replace an existing mapping entirely. This allows you to redefine how a property or behavior is handled for a specific platform or control:

```
ImageHandler.Mapper.ReplaceMapping(nameof(IconButton),
(handler, view) =>
{
    // Replace default behavior with custom logic
});
```

ModifyMapping

Similar to ReplaceMapping, this method allows you to modify an existing mapping, but instead of completely overriding it, you can change parts of the behavior:

```
ImageHandler.Mapper.ModifyMapping(nameof(IconButton), (handler,
view, action) =>
{
    // Modify existing behavior
    action?.Invoke(handler, view); // Call the original mapping
    if needed
});
```

RemoveMapping

If you want to remove a specific mapping, this method allows you to do so. It's helpful if you want to stop applying certain platform-specific behavior.

```
ImageHandler.Mapper.RemoveMapping(nameof(IconButton));
```

Preprocessor Directives

If you register mappers outside of the platform-specific folders (like Platforms/iOS), you'll need to account for platform differences. In such cases, use preprocessor directives to conditionally compile the code for each platform. For example:

```
public static class IconButtonMapper
{
    public static void MapIconButton()
    {
        ImageHandler.Mapper.AppendToMapping(nameof(IconButton),
        (handler, view) =>
        {
#if IOS
            if (view is IconButton)
            {
                handler.PlatformView.Layer.ShadowOffset = new
                CGSize(0, 3);
                handler.PlatformView.Layer.ShadowOpacity
                = 0.25f;
                handler.PlatformView.Layer.ShadowRadius = 2.0f;
                handler.PlatformView.ClipsToBounds = false;
            }
#endif

#if ANDROID
            // Android-specific shadow properties (if needed)
#endif
        });
    }
}
```

Preprocessor directives are instructions in our code that are processed before the actual compilation of the code begins and start with the # character. They allow you to conditionally include or exclude certain parts of the code depending on specific conditions, such as the platform you're targeting. This is useful when you need to write platform-specific code in a cross-platform framework, like .NET MAUI, outside of the platform-specific folders.

Common Preprocessor Directives in .NET MAUI

- #if ANDROID: Used for Android-specific code

- #if IOS: Used for iOS-specific code

- #if {Other supported platforms}: Used for that specific platform

- #else: Defines code that should run when none of the other conditions are met

- #endif: Ends the conditional block

Effects

Handlers in .NET MAUI are more powerful and customizable compared to the effects model in Xamarin.Forms. This means that, in many cases, effects might not be necessary as handlers or mappers can provide the required customization. However, effects are still supported in .NET MAUI and can be useful for lightweight, reusable functionality. Migrating your effects from Xamarin.Forms to .NET MAUI is straightforward and requires minimal changes, so you can continue using them if needed.

Our ShadowEffect was declared in the shared project and had an implementation for each platform with an attribute used by the framework to find the effect. In .NET MAUI, effects are moved to an Effects folder in the main part of the project, and the platform-specific implementation is added in the same file with conditional compilation as we discussed earlier.

This is how we declared the ShadowEffect in the shared project before:

```
/// <summary>
/// Represents a shadow effect that can be applied to UI
    elements.
/// </summary>
public class ShadowEffect : RoutingEffect
{
    /// <summary>
    /// Initializes a new instance of the <see
        cref="ShadowEffect"/> class.
    /// </summary>
    public ShadowEffect()
        : base($"AppForFitness.{nameof(ShadowEffect)}")
    {
        System.Diagnostics.Debug.WriteLine("ShadowEffect
        constructor called in shared project");
    }
}
```

And let's have a look at the Xamarin.Forms iOS implementation.
Before:

```
assembly: ResolutionGroupName("AppForFitness")]
[assembly: ExportEffect(typeof(AppForFitness.iOS.Effects.
ShadowEffect), nameof(ShadowEffect))]

namespace AppForFitness.iOS.Effects
{
    public class ShadowEffect : PlatformEffect
    {
        protected override void OnAttached()
        {
```

```
    try
    {
        var view = Container;
        if (view != null)
        {
            view.Layer.ShadowColor = UIColor.Black.
            CGColor;
            view.Layer.ShadowOffset = new CoreGraphics.
            CGSize(-2, 2);
            view.Layer.ShadowOpacity = 0.4f;
            view.Layer.ShadowRadius = 4;
        }
    }
    catch (System.Exception ex)
    {
        System.Diagnostics.Debug.WriteLine($"Cannot
        set property on attached control. Error: {ex.
        Message}");
    }
}

protected override void OnDetached()
{
}
    }
}
```

The only thing we need to do is

- Replace Xamarin.Forms with using Microsoft.Maui.
  Controls.Platform;. Chances are the Upgrade Assistant
  has already done this.

- Add the platform-specific implementations in the same file, wrapped in conditional compilation.

- Register the effect in the builder.

This is our "new" ShadowEffect:

```
using Microsoft.Maui.Controls.Platform;

#if IOS
using UIKit;
#elif ANDROID
// Add android specific references here
#endif

namespace AppForFitnessCore.Effects
{
    /// <summary>
    /// Represents a shadow effect that can be applied to UI
        elements.
    /// </summary>
    public class ShadowEffect : RoutingEffect
    {
        public ShadowEffect()
        {
            System.Diagnostics.Debug.WriteLine("ShadowEffect
            constructor called in shared project");
        }
    }
#if ANDROID
internal class PlatformShadowEffect : PlatformEffect
{
    protected override void OnAttached()
```

```
    {
// TO be implemented once we move over Android code
    }

    protected override void OnDetached()
    {
    }
}
#elif IOS
    internal class PlatformShadowEffect : PlatformEffect
    {
        protected override void OnAttached()
        {
            try
            {
                var view = Container;
                if (view != null)
                {
                    System.Diagnostics.Debug.
                    WriteLine("ShadowEffect2");

                    view.Layer.ShadowColor = UIColor.Black.
                    CGColor;
                    view.Layer.ShadowOffset = new CoreGraphics.
                    CGSize(-2, 2);
                    view.Layer.ShadowOpacity = 0.4f;
                    view.Layer.ShadowRadius = 4;
                }
            }
```

```
            catch (System.Exception ex)
            {
                System.Diagnostics.Debug.WriteLine($"Cannot
                set property on attached control. Error:
                {ex.Message}");
            }
        }

        protected override void OnDetached()
        {
            // Cleanup the control customization here
        }
    }
#endif
}
```

And the registration in the builder:

```
...
    .ConfigureMauiHandlers(handlerDelegate)
    .ConfigureFonts(fonts =>
    {
        fonts.AddFont("OpenSans-Regular.ttf",
        "OpenSansRegular");
        fonts.AddFont("OpenSans-Semibold.ttf",
        "OpenSansSemibold");
    });
builder.ConfigureEffects(effects =>
{
    effects.Add<ShadowEffect, PlatformShadowEffect>();
});
...
```

Maintaining Familiarity: Migrating Common Features

When transitioning from Xamarin to .NET MAUI, you'll find that many things remain familiar. Microsoft has aimed to keep features and patterns as consistent as possible, with only minor changes such as namespace updates. For instance, features like Xamarin.Essentials, which provided access to native device capabilities, are now built directly into .NET MAUI.

For example, if you previously used Xamarin.Essentials for secure data storage, the functionality remains largely the same. In the AppForFitness SecureStorageService.cs, we can remove the Xamarin.Essentials namespace and directly access Preferences and SecureStorage from .NET MAUI:

```
public Task StoreDataAsync(string key, string value)
{
#if DEBUG
    // Use Preferences in Debug mode since Keychain Sharing
        doesn't work with a free Apple ID.
    Preferences.Set(key, value);
    return Task.CompletedTask;
#else
    // Use SecureStorage in Release mode.
    return SecureStorage.SetAsync(key, value);
#endif
}
```

This highlights how .NET MAUI streamlines access to previously separate libraries, reducing the need for additional dependencies. Such similarities can help make the migration process smoother as many foundational concepts remain intact.

In the next chapter, we'll explore more significant changes as we dive deeper into UI migration. But before that, let's apply the same steps we used for iOS to migrate the Android platform-specific code.

Migrating the Android Code

Start by copying over the pure code folders and files from your Xamarin.Android project to the .NET MAUI Android platform folder, as well as the *Resources* folder (see Figure 7-3).

Figure 7-3. *Some of the folders and files we are copying over*

Next, move the Assets folder. We'll deal with the specifics of assets and resources in the following chapter, but for now, place them in the Android platform folder.

- Update namespaces: As we did for iOS, rename the namespaces to reflect the new structure.

- Move ShadowEffect: Combine the shadow effect code into the unified implementation for Android.

- Create IconButtonMapper: Use the logic from the old renderer to implement a custom mapper for IconButton.

- Migrate LongPressViewHandler: Refactor the long press view renderer to a handler.

- Register handlers and mappers: Add necessary registrations in MauiProgram to hook up the handlers and mappers.

- Apply minor fixes: Perform any necessary tweaks for compatibility.

Finally, consolidate the two *AndroidManifest.xml* files. Leave out the splash screen for now, as we'll address this in the next chapter.

Once you've migrated one platform, you'll find it somewhat easier to migrate the others. However, with the exception of handling renderers, I have to note that working on the UI has been the most time-consuming part for me and my colleagues.

Summary

In this chapter, we tackled the migration of platform-specific projects, focusing first on iOS, followed by Android. We discussed how, after migrating the shared project, many apps may still be incomplete or even fail to build due to missing platform-specific code. We explored how to address this by migrating platform logic and handling dependencies, such as temporary implementations for services, and other quick fixes that we have to address later.

We also delved into key changes in .NET MAUI, such as how the Handler pattern has replaced the renderer pattern from Xamarin.Forms. The chapter highlighted the migration of specific components to handlers while introducing the concept of mappers. At the end of the chapter, the AppForFitness app is building, but a lot of work remains. However, with the foundation from this chapter and the last and our inventory, we are ready to dive into assets, resources, UI design, navigation, and splash screens in the next chapter.

CHAPTER 8

Migrating the UI and Navigation

The AppForFitness app is somewhat functional at this stage, but visually there is a lot of work to be done. The styling still looks off, and platform-specific discrepancies are affecting the appearance and behavior of certain controls. For example, our layout controls are rendering differently, and some styling was lost during migration. These styling issues are minor tweaks, in particular as .NET MAUI has unified a lot of the control styling, which means we need less customization to ensure a consistent look and feel across all platforms.

In addition, we still don't have a splash screen, haven't fully addressed resources, and haven't fixed the styling for various UI elements. Since tweaking the visual appearance is mostly a matter of fine-tuning, we'll save styling for last and instead focus on one of the most significant improvements in .NET MAUI: navigation.

.NET MAUI has introduced a more efficient and streamlined navigation system compared to Xamarin.Forms, and we want to leverage these enhancements to our advantage in the AppForFitness app.

© Iris Classon 2025
I. Classon, *Migrating from Xamarin.Forms to .NET MAUI*,
https://doi.org/10.1007/979-8-8688-1215-6_8

AppShell and Navigation

The current navigation in the AppForFitness app feels like an afterthought, which is often the case in legacy applications. During our inventory, we listed the places we navigate, some of them in need of improvement. Now, as we revisit navigation, that inventory will help us streamline and modernize it.

For reference, here are the findings from our inventory:

- MainPage uses tabs for navigation.

- ProgressPage navigates via Navigation.PushAsync with parameters.

- EntryPage navigates with Navigation.PushAsync but without parameters.

- There are two custom pop-ups implemented.

- There is also deep link navigation to EntryPage using Navigation.PushAsync with parameters.

In .NET MAUI, navigation has been significantly simplified and enhanced. The Shell consolidates the various navigation approaches into a unified, flexible model. Shell in .NET MAUI is essentially an evolution of the Shell that was introduced in Xamarin.Forms 4.x, but with several improvements and refinements, especially around performance, flexibility, and usability. Shell navigation includes URI-based navigation, similar to that of a website, which means we don't have to follow a set hierarchy. This also means it's easier to add to an existing application without having to redo everything. We've already used Shell in our EntryPage:

```
await Shell.Current.GoToAsync(nameof(ProgressPage));
```

but kept the Navigation.PushAsync on our ProgressPage:

```
private void OnEntryButtonClicked(object sender, EventArgs e)
{
    if (sender is Button button)
    {
        Navigation.PushAsync(new EntryPage(button.Text));
    }
}
```

We certainly don't want to mix the two, and using GoToAsync with Shell is our best approach. Shell has PushAsync, which uses stack-based navigation. However, GoToAsync is more flexible. When you navigate using GoToAsync(), it still maintains a navigation stack under the hood works on top of the navigation stack, but with added flexibility through route-based navigation.

Let's clean up our navigation!

AppForFitness Navigation

To improve the navigation structure, we'll make the following changes:

- Replace the TabbedPage in MainPage with AppShell. This will allow us to manage navigation and tabs more declaratively and make future extensions easier.

- Use Shell URI–based navigation for managing page transitions and parameters, instead of using Navigation.PushAsync or Shell.Current.PushAsync.

- Deep linking will be integrated into AppShell's routing system to simplify the way users are taken directly to the EntryPage with relevant parameters.

We'll kick things off by reintroducing the AppShell.XAML that we removed earlier in the migration, and we'll add our tabs there:

```xml
<?xml version="1.0" encoding="UTF-8" ?>
<Shell
    x:Class="AppForFitnessCore.AppShell"
    xmlns="http://schemas.microsoft.com/dotnet/2021/maui"
    xmlns:x="http://schemas.microsoft.com/winfx/2009/xaml"
    xmlns:views="clr-namespace:AppForFitnessCore.Views"
    Title="App For Fitness">
    <Shell.ToolbarItems>
        <ToolbarItem Text="App For Fitness" >
        </ToolbarItem>
        <ToolbarItem Text="✉"
                     Clicked="OnEmailClicked" >
        </ToolbarItem>
        <ToolbarItem Text="🌐"
                     Clicked="OnLanguageSettingsClicked" >
        </ToolbarItem>
    </Shell.ToolbarItems>
    <TabBar>
        <ShellContent
            Title="Progress"
            ContentTemplate="{DataTemplate
            views:ProgressPage}"/>
        <ShellContent
            Title="New Entry"
            ContentTemplate="{DataTemplate views:EntryPage}"/>
        <ShellContent
            Title="Settings"
```

```
        ContentTemplate="{DataTemplate
        views:SettingsPage}"/>
    </TabBar>
</Shell>
```

The code-behind file looks the same as MainPage.cs, but I suspect that our pop-up doesn't need the current complicated logic that it has. Due to TabbedPage limitations with adding a control on top of it, we had to create a grid, insert the content, and overlay the pop-up. We'll get back to this as soon as we're done with the navigation. The AppShell is then added to the App.cs constructor.

Before:

```
MainPage = new NavigationPage(new MainPage());
```

Now:

```
MainPage = new AppShell();
```

With that in place, we can remove MainPage, test the application, commit, and push.

How does this work? The ShellContent elements within the TabBar automatically create implicit routes based on the titles of the content. However, if you pass parameters, then you have to explicitly register the route. EntryPage has two constructors, and one of them has a parameter.

The routes, when explicitly defined, usually look like this:

```
Routing.RegisterRoute("somepage", typeof(SomePage));
```

or like this:

```
Routing.RegisterRoute(nameof(SomePage), typeof(SomePage));
```

Note   While the second option makes sure the routes are updated if the cage name changes, it does create a dependency whenever we navigate to that page. Declaring constants using nameof will also create transitive dependencies. However, the best way to deal with this is outside the scope of this book, so for now we'll use nameOf().

Let's change all the navigation code to URI-based navigation. For example, ProgressPage.cs will navigate like this:

```
private async void OnEntryButtonClicked(object sender,
EventArgs e)
{
    if (sender is Button button)
    {
        var exerciseName = Uri.EscapeDataString(button.Text);
        await      Shell.Current.GoToAsync($"//{nameof
        (EntryPage)}?exerciseName={exerciseName}");
    }
}
```

"//" is used to reset the navigation stack entirely and navigate to the new route as the "root" of the stack. This is useful when you want to navigate to a page without keeping a history of the previous navigations.

We can also use QueryProperties (introduced in Xamarin.Forms 4.3 as part of the Shell navigation improvements) instead of using the constructor of a class:

```
[QueryProperty(nameof(ExerciseName), Config.RouteParams.
exerciseName)]
public partial class EntryPage
{
    private string _exerciseName;
```

```
public string ExerciseName
{
    get => _exerciseName;
    set
    {
        if (_exerciseName != value)
        {
            _exerciseName = Uri.UnescapeDataString(value);
            if (!string.IsNullOrEmpty(ExerciseName) &&
            ExercisePicker.Items.Any())
            {
                ExercisePicker.SelectedIndex = _exercises.
                FindIndex(x => x.Name == ExerciseName);
            }
        }
    }
}
```

This frees up the constructor from query parameters and leaves space (metaphorically speaking) to inject dependencies instead. I've added UnescapeString since we'll be passing in the parameter through external query parameters.

EntryPage uses the FitnessApiService, like we discussed earlier, we can use dependency injection to inject dependencies.

If we register the page and FitnessApiService in the service collection, and the query parameter is defined as a QueryProperty, then everything just happens by magic:

```
public EntryPage(FitnessApiService apiService)
{
    _apiService = apiService;
    InitializeComponent();
}
```

and in the builder:

```
builder.Services.AddTransient<FitnessApiService>();
builder.Services.AddTransient<EntryPage>();
```

If we want to clean this up even more, we can define our magic strings in the config file:

```
/// <summary>
/// Contains route parameter constants used for deep linking
and navigation within the application.
/// </summary>
public static class RouteParams
{
    /// <summary>
    /// The exercise name route param.
    /// </summary>
    public const string exerciseName = nameof(exerciseName);
}
```

and use them like this:

```
await Shell.Current.GoToAsync($"///{nameof(EntryPage)}?{Config.
RouteParams.exerciseName}={escapedExerciseName}");
```

Deep Linking

When we sorted out our navigation, we even sorted out our deep link navigation without much work. Unfortunately, I ran into some problems with my deep linking, and although in theory you should be able to just handle them in App.xaml.cs in the OnAppLinkRequestReceived method, I was redirected to the app but not the specific page, and the method was never called. I solved this by catching the routing in the platform-specific entry points (you can see the solution in Appendix B), but I'm hoping this issue is resolved by the time the book comes out.

In addition, I cleaned up my Android manifest and moved my intents to the MainActivity and removed one that is not in use.

Community Toolkit: Popup

In our inventory list, we added the pop-up navigation as well. TabbedPage in Xamarin.Forms is special, and adding an overlay is tricky, and therefore we had an elaborate and error-prone solution. We could redo it for .NET MAUI and remove workarounds for the TabbedPage which we aren't using anymore. I've opted to use the MAUI Community Toolkit for the pop-up instead (the MAUI version of the Xamarin Toolkit), which is simply done by adding the NuGet package, registering it in the builder:

```
builder
    .UseMauiApp<App>()
    .UseMauiCompatibility()
    .UseSkiaSharp()
    .UseOxyPlotSkia()
    .UseMauiCommunityToolkit()
```

and implementing the logic:

```
public class PopupService
{
    private readonly Popup _popup = new()
    {
        Size = new Size(300, 300),
        Color = Colors.White
    };

    public async Task ShowEmailPopup(Page currentPage)
    {
        _popup.Content = new StackLayout
        {
...
```

The Popup class handles all the logic, similar to our previous PopupLayout implementation which I removed after adding the Community Toolkit.

This brings us to an issue with Shell.ToolBarItems. At the time of writing, the toolbar items are not displayed on iOS. There are a couple of workarounds, but I opted to use the items in the Shell.TitleView. You can read more about the bug and workarounds later in the book.

TitleView code:

```
<Shell.TitleView>
    <HorizontalStackLayout HorizontalOptions="End">
        <Button Text="✉"
                Clicked="OnEmailClicked"/>
        <Button Text="🌐"
            Clicked="OnLanguageSettingsClicked"/>
    </HorizontalStackLayout>
</Shell.TitleView>
```

Managing Platform Differences

Platform differences can be handled by either finding a workaround that works for all targeted platforms or by providing platform-specific implementations like we did for our handlers. Our chart isn't working at the moment, and that is due to our temporary service registration for fetching the user ID which we added as a temporary solution before we migrated the platform code for the two targeted platforms.

Just as I did with the handlers, I've now added a delegate to register platform-specific service registrations. You can, of course, choose to keep platform-specific registrations in the MainProgram.cs file (or other shared location) and use conditional compilation to include/exclude based on platform. Personally, I prefer some separation of control, even though we do run the risk of missing a registration for a platform. We could use reflection to auto-register or use partial classes and so on. The options are many; .NET MAUI and .NET in general are very flexible. Do what works for your solution.

Layouts

If you've run the AppForFitness at this point in the migration, or migrated your own application, you've probably noticed that while the app might work it certainly looks different. We touched on this earlier in the book, how layouts and controls are a little bit different in .NET MAUI; here are some (but not all) differences. From here on, we'll refer to "controls" as views as layout controls are also controls. Views, commonly referred to as controls or widgets, are UI objects such as buttons, borders, images, and so on. They often have a specific user purpose. In this book, we will be focusing on layouts, although some views will get a special mention, for example, Border. Here is a recap from earlier, regarding some layout and view changes:

- Default layout values: In .NET MAUI, padding, margins, and spacing default to zero, unlike in Xamarin.Forms. To maintain previous behavior, we can use implicit styles.

- Frame: While Frame is still supported, it is recommended that you use the Border control for more uniform padding and behavior across platforms.

- Grid: Unlike Xamarin.Forms, .NET MAUI requires explicit declaration of rows and columns.

- StackLayout: StackLayout's behavior is now more predictable, and new options like VerticalStackLayout and HorizontalStackLayout are introduced, with a recommendation to use Grid for layouts that need space subdivision. There's also some additional layout differences in terms of using available space that I'll address later.

- RelativeLayout: Its usage is discouraged, and it's only available via the compatibility package. Use Grid whenever possible.

- ScrollView: ScrollView now automatically expands to fit its content, which can cause unexpected behavior, especially in layouts like VerticalStackLayout that allow infinite growth.

One notable change in .NET MAUI layouts, especially compared to Xamarin.Forms, is how layouts expand and handle available space.

Infinite Expansion

In .NET MAUI, layouts like `VerticalStackLayout` and `HorizontalStackLayout` can expand infinitely to accommodate their child elements, unlike Xamarin.Forms where the layout would sometimes stop expanding based on the available screen space or parent control.

ScrollView

For some views, such as ScrollView, this can be problematic. Since it can grow indefinitely, the ScrollView may expand to fit all content, resulting in different behavior from your Xamarin.Forms app. You'll need to add constraints or adjust child elements if this is a problem. There are also a few issues that at the time of writing haven't been solved yet, for example, shadow property not being applied to content inside the ScrollView. See the Appendix B for examples.

*AndExpand

Properties like FillAndExpand, commonly used in StackLayout in Xamarin. Forms, are either ignored or behave differently in VerticalStackLayout and HorizontalStackLayout. Use Grid for more precise control over space distribution when dealing with expanding content.

The layout engine has been redone, so we'd have more predictable layout behavior in .NET MAUI in terms of how child elements are arranged and sized. And while this is helpful when dealing with complex layouts, it also means we need to rethink our layouts and adjust post-migration.

UI Advice

Many of the problems my team encountered with layouts and controls were related to mixing .NET MAUI and .NET MAUI Compatibility pack. The Compatibility package is meant to help the transition to .NET MAUI, and therefore my recommendation is that you try to use it as little as possible, if at all.

Given the differences between Xamarin.Forms and .NET MAUI, here are a few migration tips to get you started:

- If possible, remove reliance on the Compatibility package. Use the suggestions below to get there.

- Replace StackLayout: Consider using VerticalStackLayout and HorizontalStackLayout instead of StackLayout. When more complex layouts are needed, use Grid for better control and performance.

- Move away from RelativeLayout: Replace RelativeLayout with Grid or other layout containers.

- Reevaluate usage of AbsoluteLayout: Although .NET MAUI includes this control, it should be regarded as a special-purpose layout. It adds to the complexity of a layout and can have unpredictable results due to different screen sizes and densities across devices. In addition, it is very CPU intensive and can result in performance issues.

- Remove *AndExpand properties: Remove any use of FillAndExpand or similar properties, as these are no longer supported in the new stack layouts. While they won't cause build errors, they will be ignored.

- Transition from Frame to Border: Where possible, replace Frame with Border for more consistent styling and padding behavior.

- Explicitly declare Grid rows and columns: Update any grids to explicitly declare RowDefinitions and ColumnDefinitions, as the auto-inferred layout behavior has been removed.

An extra note on StackLayouts: When you nest these, the more layout calculations will be performed. This can and probably will impact performance. Use a Grid instead of trying to recreate one using other layout controls (or views).

We'll use that list to address the layouts in AppForFitness. Here are some changes made to AppForFitness.

I used Find Usages for StackLayout (Figures 8-1 and 8-2) and the orientation property so I could replace the StackLayout with HorizontalStackLayout or VerticalStackLayout.

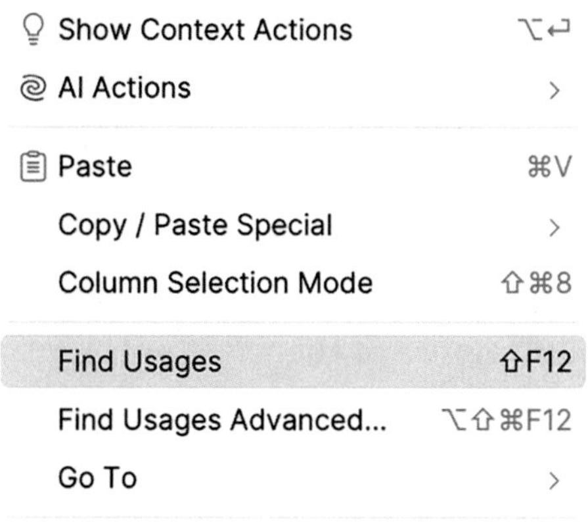

Show Context Actions ⌥↵

AI Actions >

Paste ⌘V

Copy / Paste Special >

Column Selection Mode ⇧⌘8

Find Usages ⇧F12

Find Usages Advanced... ⌥⇧⌘F12

Go To >

Figure 8-1. *Find Usages is a handy feature in many IDEs and lets us find usages of a type or member*

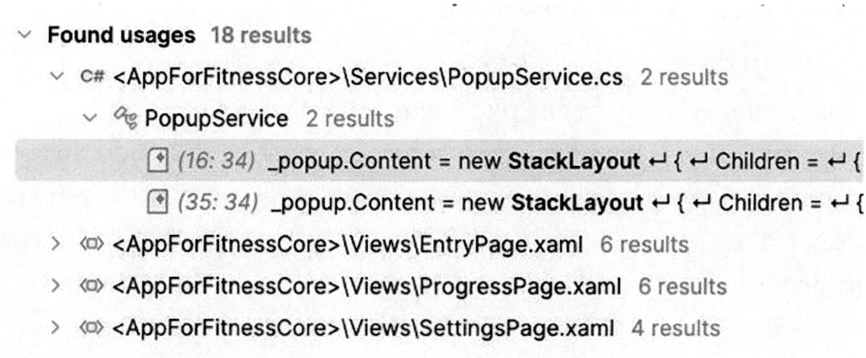

∨ **Found usages** 18 results

  ∨ C# <AppForFitnessCore>\Services\PopupService.cs 2 results

    ∨ PopupService 2 results

      (16: 34) _popup.Content = new **StackLayout** ↵ { ↵ Children = ↵ {

      (35: 34) _popup.Content = new **StackLayout** ↵ { ↵ Children = ↵ {

  > <AppForFitnessCore>\Views\EntryPage.xaml 6 results

  > <AppForFitnessCore>\Views\ProgressPage.xaml 6 results

  > <AppForFitnessCore>\Views\SettingsPage.xaml 4 results

Figure 8-2. *AppForFitness has several StackLayouts*

When I started changing all my StackLayout to either horizontal or vertical on the EntryPage.xaml, I realized that I was using the stack views as rows and columns. So instead I defined a grid with rows and columns and added the child views there. Previously, I had used Frame with a custom effect to add a specific shadow (Frame in Xamarin.Forms has a shadow property, but we'll pretend we wanted something else done with the shadow). This has been replaced with the Border control, which wraps the content of the ContentPage, with an added top padding so the TitleView in the Shell which is layered on top won't look like it's on top. .NET MAUI has a shadow property for the controls (and views), which means unless we want something very specific, or specific behavior for a platform, we can remove the custom effects.

A search in all files for "AndExpand" helped me locate references to *AndExpand so I could remove or change layout properties.

The LanguagePicker was also refactored to use a VerticalStackLayout, and the PopupService which now uses a third-party pop-up view wraps the pop-up content in a Border view so we can get the same rounded edges we had in the previous pop-up implementation.

Assets and Resources

.NET MAUI simplifies image management by centralizing image and resource management in one place, with resizing handled by NET MAUI. You can still have platform-specific images, but you'll find that the majority of resources can be shared and therefor placed in one location, Resources/Images. Use the inventory we did earlier to identify images that are identical visually and that don't need platform-specific versions. Let's take a look at the changes made in AppForFitness.

Images

Our background image, bg.png, was in the shared project and was migrated to the Resources/Images folder in the .NET MAUI project, but the dumbbell image is still duplicated, once for each platform. I've now moved it to the Resources/Images.

Note   Keep in mind that SVG files are converted to PNGs, so use the .png extension when referencing them in your app. Additionally, image names should be lowercase containing only alphanumeric characters or underscores and start and end with a letter character. This is an Android requirement.

When you add images to a project, you can do so by dragging and dropping or by adding an item. If you add an image to the Resource/Images folder, the build action should be set to MauiImage; however, I've noticed that the Upgrade Assistant doesn't always do that, so you want to double-check by taking a look at the image properties (right-click ➤ Properties).

MauiImage BaseSize

.NET MAUI lets you set a base size for an image in the project file by setting the BaseSize and Resize attribute. The BaseSize attribute helps us define a logical size that the image will use as a basis for resizing. This can be useful when working with, for example, a background image or thumbnail image that needs to scale properly across different screen sizes and aspect ratios.

The BaseSize defines the "logical" dimensions that the image is going to be treated as before it is resized based on the actual screen size. The values in BaseSize should correspond to the aspect ratio of your original image to avoid distortion.

In our case, if we want to set a new base size to the background image, which is 1242 × 2688, and we want to maintain its aspect ratio across various devices, the BaseSize should be something close to this, but scaled down to a logical size that works well for the screen resolution and performance.

For example:

```
<MauiImage Include="Resources\Images\bg.png" Resize="True"
BaseSize="414,896"/>
```

However, this won't sort out our background image issue in AppForFitness, which shows a distorted image. Just as with Xamarin. Forms, in .NET MAUI, the BackgroundImageSource does not automatically scale the image by itself, and there's no aspect ratio property we can use. It uses the image "as is," meaning it renders the image at its original resolution, regardless of the device's screen size. The options are the same as for our premigrated app:

- Replace image with a background brush

- Use a control to wrap content and set background image on that control

- Dynamically but manually create or use images with size matching the device

You can see an example for the first option in the AppForFitness repository, and I've left one page as before, but with a new base size. Creating and using a gradient brush is the same in .NET MAUI as in Xamarin.Forms.

Icons

Continuing on the topic of image management, managing icon assets is also a whole lot easier now. For example, you no longer need to manually handle Assets.xcassets the same way you would in a Xamarin. Forms project. Instead, MAUI centralizes image handling and simplifies it through the Resources/Images directory as mentioned earlier. MAUI will automatically resize images for different platforms without needing you to manually create multiple image versions for different resolutions. For example, it will create the appropriate image sizes for Android (hdpi, xhdpi, xxhdpi, etc.) and iOS (@1x, @2x, @3x).

To add an app icon in .NET MAUI:

1. Add the icon: Place your image in the `Resources\`
    `AppIcon` folder (or similar). Supported formats
    include PNG, JPG, and SVG.

2. Declare in project file: Add the icon in the `.csproj`
    file using

    ```
    <ItemGroup>
        <MauiIcon Include="Resources\AppIcon/
        appicon.svg" />
    </ItemGroup>
    ```

    You can set different icons depending on the
    platform by using the Condition attribute:

    ```
    Condition="$([MSBuild]::GetTargetPlatformIdentifier
    ('$(TargetFramework)')) == 'windows'"
    ```

3. Composed icons: To use separate background and
    foreground images, specify the ForegroundFile:

    ```
    <MauiIcon Include="Resources/AppIcon/appiconbg.png"
    ForegroundFile="Resources/AppIcon/appiconfg.svg" />
    ```

4. Set base size (optional): Define the base size for
    bitmaps:

    ```
    <MauiIcon Include="Resources/AppIcon/appicon.png"
    BaseSize="128,128" />
    ```

5. iOS: Add to Info.plist.

    ```
        <key>XSAppIconAssets</key>
    <string>Assets.xcassets/appicon.appiconset</string>
    ```

And for Android:

```
<application
        android:allowBackup="true"
        android:icon="@mipmap/appicon"
        android:roundIcon="@mipmap/appicon_round"
```

Clean the solution, and uninstall the app, before building and deploying.

Splash Screen

As with images and icons, splash screens are straightforward to implement unless you want to do something more complex, for example, animations.

Steps:

1. Add a splash screen image to Resources/Splash and set build action MauiSplashScreen.

2. Add to the csproj file.

3. For iOS, add to info.plist:

    ```
    <key>UILaunchStoryboardName</key>
    <string>MauiSplash</string>
    ```

4. For Android, add to MainActivity:

    ```
    [Activity(Theme = "@style/Maui.SplashTheme",
    MainLauncher = true, ConfigurationChanges
    = ConfigChanges.ScreenSize | ConfigChanges.
    Orientation | ConfigChanges.UiMode |
    ConfigChanges.ScreenLayout | ConfigChanges.
    SmallestScreenSize)]
    ```

```
    public class MainActivity : MauiAppCompatActivity
```
For iOS 15 and up the app must be signed for the
app to load the splash screen, add, for example
something like:

```
<PropertyGroup Condition="'$(Configuration)'=='Debug'">
    <EnableCodeSigning>true</EnableCodeSigning>
    <CodesignProvisioningProfile>iOS Development
    Profile</CodesignProvisioningProfile>
    <CodesignRequireProvisioningProfile>true</
    CodesignRequireProvisioningProfile>
</PropertyGroup>
```

```
<PropertyGroup Condition="'$(Configuration)'=='
Release'">
    <EnableCodeSigning>true</EnableCodeSigning>
    <CodesignProvisioningProfile>iOS Distribution
    Profile</CodesignProvisioningProfile>
    <CodesignRequireProvisioningProfile>true</
    CodesignRequireProvisioningProfile>
    <CodesignTeamIdentifier>YOUR_TEAM_ID</
    CodesignTeamIdentifier>
</PropertyGroup>
```

After moving images and icons and creating the splash screen, build
and run the app. If everything works and looks as expected, go ahead and
remove the folder and files we moved over from the old platform projects
that are no longer needed. For example, I've deleted my drawable folders
for Android and the assets folder for iOS.

Styling

Styling is what adds that extra oomph to an app, and thankfully .NET MAUI has continued to build on the flexible and powerful styling options in Xamarin.Forms. Even more so now that we can centralize styling yet cater for platform differences with OnPlatform in XAML or conditional compilation.

```
<Style TargetType="Label">
    <Setter Property="BackgroundColor">
        <Setter.Value>
            <OnPlatform x:TypeArguments="Color">
                <On Platform="iOS" Value="Crimson" />
                <On Platform="Android" Value="Yellow" />
            </OnPlatform>
        </Setter.Value>
    </Setter>
</Style>
```

Likewise, CSS styling has improved. CSS in .NET MAUI works seamlessly (mostly) with new controls and views introduced in the framework, unlike Xamarin.Forms where some controls had limited CSS support.

CSS styling is added by adding a stylesheet to the Styles folder, making sure build action is set to MauiCSS, and referencing it where you want to use it. Fully styling a .NET MAUI app using CSS alone is not possible, but you can combine CSS and XAML.

CSS example:

```
.titleViewButton{
    background-color: transparent;
    color: #3b9651;
}
```

```
<ContentPage.Resources>
    <StyleSheet Source="/Resources/Styles/styles.css" />
</ContentPage.Resources>
```

Specifying class:

```
<Shell.TitleView>
    <HorizontalStackLayout HorizontalOptions="End"
    HeightRequest="50">
        <Button class="titleViewButton" Text="✉"
                Clicked="OnEmailClicked"/>
        <Button class="titleViewButton" Text="🌐"
            Clicked="OnLanguageSettingsClicked"/>
    </HorizontalStackLayout>
</Shell.TitleView>
```

.NET MAUI has also improved styling options for controls and views, for example, you can now easily set TabbedPage colors using properties directly in XAML or C# without needing a platform-specific handler or renderer like we had in the original implementation.

For example:

```
<TabbedPage BarBackgroundColor="LightGray"
            BarTextColor="Black"
            SelectedTabColor="Blue"
            UnselectedTabColor="Gray">
    <ContentPage Title="Home" />
    <ContentPage Title="Settings" />
</TabbedPage>
```

Styling Limitations

It's frustrating, but at some point, we will run into problems with styling MAUI Views and Controls. For example, at the time of writing, while I can style some aspects of the Shell and ShellContent, some properties do not exist and can't be styled. Nor is there a handler we can use.

I've set the same style for the background and foreground colors on the tab items, but changing font size was not available out of the box. The reorganization of the Shell and NavigationPage components into Handlers is not yet complete. Our option at this point would be to reintroduce the compatibility pack and use the ShellRenderer or create our own Shell navigation.

Whenever you come across an issue, bug, or limitation, please submit an issue to the .NET MAUI repository. More on that in Appendix B.

Note   If your styling isn't showing, make sure to check the Styles. xaml file if you have one. The default for .NET MAUI declares a lot of styles. Do a search for the property in your project; you might be surprised to find several declarations sprinkled throughout. Generally, it's better to stick to styling declarations in resource dictionaries than incline styling. If you use an AI assistant with your IDE, for example, Rider AI assistant, GitHub Copilot, or Augment plugin, you can ask the AI assistant to locate incline styling and help refactor to centralize styling.

Shadows

I've spent a lot of time on shadow in Xamarin.Forms, and I'm very happy about the improvements in .NET MAUI. As mentioned earlier, there is now a shadow property on views and controls.

In .NET MAUI, shadows are applied to the outline or boundary of the child elements, not the parent layout, for example, a VerticalStackLayout, which we used before wrapping it in a Border control. Therefore, even though you are applying a shadow to the VerticalStackLayout, the shadow will be drawn around the layout's content and not the layout frame itself.

The Shadow is applied to the content inside the layout, but not the entire layout's boundary as the layout itself doesn't have a "visual presence" (frame or border) to cast a shadow. Only the child elements inside the layout do.

This actually works in our favor. AppForFitness has a custom IconButton that sets a shadow on a transparent image. The Android handler uses a custom outline provider to create the shadow which was causing some lag when the page was rendered. We can now remove the custom view, handler, and outline provider. In addition, by using the shadow style we defined for our other shadows, we can get a more cohesive look.

Summary

In this chapter, we finalized the AppForFitness migration, focusing on visual design and navigation improvements. We revamped the navigation by transitioning to Shell, leveraging URI-based routes for simpler and more flexible navigation management.

We also dealt with styling as some was lost during migration, .NET MAUI's unified styling has greatly reduced the need for platform-specific customization, and we've used that to our advantage while also discussing existing issues and controls that lack styling options.

We also updated layouts, switching from Frame to Border and replacing StackLayout with more efficient alternatives like VerticalStackLayout and HorizontalLayout and replacing RelativeLayout with Grid. Image and asset management has been unified, and we addressed splash screen and app icon improvements. We are almost done, but first let's do some cleaning up and focus on removing obsolete code, improving performance and memory usage and accessibility.

CHAPTER 9

Cleaning Up, Testing, and Optimization

We've successfully migrated the app, but there's one more crucial step: cleaning up, optimizing, and testing. When it comes to mobile apps, performant and robust apps are everything. Users expect apps to be snappy, responsive, quick to load, and mostly bug-free. If those expectations aren't met, they're likely to leave quickly, possibly with a negative review.

In this chapter, I'll dive into ways to ensure your .NET MAUI app doesn't just work but works fast and efficiently while future-proofing by removing obsolete code and adding tests.

Removing Obsolete Code

As we've discussed earlier in the book, there are quite a few namespaces, types, and members that are now obsolete in .NET MAUI. So far, we've focused on areas like the *ExpandAll layout properties, but it's important to clean up any other outdated code as well.

If you're using Rider for development, you'll notice that it doesn't have a group by type option in the Problems window, which could make it tricky to identify all obsolete code in one go. However, there's a quick workaround: you can search for the following problem codes in your Solution Files (Figure 9-1):

- CS0618: This warning indicates the use of an obsolete
  API with a replacement suggestion, making it easier for
  you to update.

- CS0612: This warning indicates the use of an obsolete
  API without a replacement suggestion, meaning
  you'll need to dig a bit deeper to find an appropriate
  alternative.

Additionally, it's a good idea to double-check for any missed obsolete code by searching for the word "obsolete" across your project. This ensures nothing gets left behind during cleanup and helps prevent future issues with outdated functionality.

Figure 9-1. *You can search for the obsolete error code to locate warnings for obsolete types or members*

MessageCenter

The first obsolete type we are going to address is MessageCenter. This is the warning description, which even includes recommended replacement:

'Microsoft.Maui.Controls.MessagingCenter' is obsolete: 'We recommend migrating to `CommunityToolkit.Mvvm.Messaging. WeakReferenceMessenger`'.

MessageCenter had several limitations, such as lack of strong typing, limited scalability, and most of all an easy way to introduce memory leaks. Replacing it is straightforward as the replacement follows the same messenger pattern. Here are the steps:

1. Add the CommunityToolkit.Mvvm NuGet package.

2. Create a message type for the language changed messages:

    ```
    public class LanguageChangedMessage(string value) :
    ValueChangedMessage<string>(value);
    ```

3. Register recipient for the message in OnAppearing:

    ```
    protected override async void OnAppearing()
    {
        base.OnAppearing();
        WeakReferenceMessenger.Default.Register
        <LanguageChangedMessage>(this, OnLanguageChanged);
    // Code omitted
    }

    private void OnLanguageChanged(object recipient,
    LanguageChangedMessage message)
    {
    ```

```
plotLabel.Text = string.Format(Appres.ProgressText,
    _defaultMainMuscle.Name, _currentFormula.
    ToString());
}
```

4. Unregister in the OnDisappearing:

```
protected override void OnDisappearing()
{
    base.OnDisappearing();
    WeakReferenceMessenger.Default.Unregister
    <LanguageChangedMessage>(this);
}
```

5. Send message in the LanguagePicker:

```
private void OnLanguageChanged(object sender,
EventArgs e)
{
// Code omitted
            WeakReferenceMessenger.Default.Send
            (new LanguageChangedMessage
            (selectedLanguage));
        }
    }
}
```

6. Remove MessageCenter usage from code.

Run the app; confirm the changes work as intended. Commit the changes to source control.

Thread Management

Our next two warnings are related to threading and the Device object.
Microsoft.Maui.Controls.Device is obsolete. Instead, we can use
DeviceInfo.

For example, our SecureStorageService had platform-specific
implementations as keychain sharing does not work with a free Apple
ID. Therefore, for debug we wanted to use Preferences to store data.
By using DeviceInfo, we can consolidate the SecureStorageService
implementations like this:

```
public async Task StoreDataAsync(string key, string value)
{
    try
    {
        if (DeviceInfo.Platform == DevicePlatform.iOS &&
        Debugger.IsAttached)
        {
            // Use Preferences in Debug mode for iOS. Keychain
                Sharing does not work with a free Apple ID.
            Preferences.Set(key, value);
        }
        else
        {
            await SecureStorage.SetAsync(key, value);
        }
    }
// Code omitted
```

.BeginInvokeOnMainThread(Action) is also obsolete. The warning tells us what to do: 'Use BindableObject.Dispatcher.Dispatch() instead.' We can replace this:

```
Device.BeginInvokeOnMainThread(() => plotView.Model = _
plotModel);
```

with this:

```
Dispatcher.Dispatch(() => plotView.Model = _plotModel);
```

Using Dispatcher.Dispatch is optimal for classes that have access to a Dispatcher (like pages, views, and other classes that inherit from BindableObject), as it provides synchronous, main-thread dispatching for quick, direct UI updates. However, in contexts where a Dispatcher might not be available—such as view models or services—you can use MainThread.InvokeOnMainThreadAsync from Microsoft.Maui.Essentials:

```
await MainThread.InvokeOnMainThreadAsync(() => DoStuff());
```

MainThread.InvokeOnMainThreadAsync is an asynchronous alternative that automatically checks if the code is already on the main thread and only dispatches if necessary, making it useful in non-UI-bound contexts. You can use the MainThread.IsMainThread property if you want to explicitly check if you are on the main thread.

For example:

```
Debug.WriteLine($"Im on main: {MainThread.IsMainThread}");
```

Our AutomationProperties.* on SettingsPage are also obsolete although there's no warning in the Problems window in Rider. We'll address the properties in the Accessibility in ".NET MAUI" section.

Here is a list of other types and members that are obsolete in .NET MAUI 8 and 9:

- TargetIdiom

- FocusRequest

- MauiImageView

- RootPanel

- MauiTimePicker.DateSelected

- Entry.ControlsEntryMapper

- Layout.Mapper

- Picker.Mapper

- WebView.Mapper

- And many more *.Mapper. Use the handler instead.

- IFontNamedSizeService

- AcceleratorTypeConverter

- PopupManager

- ControlsSwipeMapper

- ControlsToolbarMapper

- SearchBar.MapIsSpellCheckEnabled

- ControlsFlyoutPageMapper

- ControlsScrollViewMapper

- UiContainerView

- FormsTextView.ctr with params

- GradientShader

- LinearGradientShader

- ClickGestureRecognizer.cs

- TemplateBinding

- MessagingCenter.cs

- *AndExpand

- AutomationProperties.*

After cleaning up the obsolete types and members, I decided to take it a step further and perform some general cleanup to remove leftover warnings and improve the overall clarity of the project. One of the best practices I use regularly is the quick action feature that I mentioned earlier in the book. This tool is incredibly helpful for tasks like removing unused namespaces, renaming variables for clarity, and refactoring code.

It's tempting to ignore warnings, especially when they don't seem critical. However, these warnings have a habit of multiplying over time, leading to a cluttered solution that's hard to manage. By addressing them immediately, you prevent potential issues from snowballing. Cleaning them up as they arise will keep the project organized and reduce technical debt down the road.

Our team has found that using a linter or configuring the project to treat warnings as errors helps to keep the codebase clean and warning-free. This practice encourages everyone to pay attention to the details and not just the high-level architecture. It also fosters a culture of continuous improvement, where small optimizations lead to a more maintainable and professional project.

Accessibility in .NET MAUI

Up until now, we've largely overlooked the accessibility features in our app, particularly on the SettingsPage where we declared automation properties. However, accessibility is a critical aspect of app development, and .NET MAUI has significantly improved in this area with the introduction of semantic properties (previously referred to as automation properties). These properties make it easier to ensure that your app is accessible to users who rely on assistive technologies like screen readers.

Obsolete Automation Properties

In .NET MAUI, several of the old automation properties are now obsolete, including

- `AutomationProperties.Name`

- `AutomationProperties.HelpText`

- `AutomationProperties.LabeledBy`

Depending on the IDE you use, you might not receive warnings for these obsolete properties, so it's important to be proactive in replacing them with their modern equivalents.

Using Semantic Properties

The new SemanticProperties in .NET MAUI provide more flexibility and clarity for accessibility features, helping users who utilize screen readers or other assistive technologies. Here are some key properties:

- SemanticProperties.Description: This property provides a detailed description of an element. It serves the same purpose as AutomationProperties.Name, offering context to users about the function or content of the element.

171

- SemanticProperties.Hint: This property offers additional guidance on how to interact with the element, similar to AutomationProperties.HelpText. It is especially useful for elements like buttons or text fields, where a user might need instructions on how to use them.

- SemanticProperties.HeadingLevel: This property indicates the heading level of text, helping users navigate hierarchical content, such as headings or sections. This is a new addition that didn't exist with the previous automation properties.

One element can also provide accessibility information for another. For example, a Label next to a Picker can explain the purpose of the Picker by linking the two elements through accessibility properties. This provides extra clarity for users who rely on screen readers to understand the context of different UI elements.

Additional Considerations

When implementing accessibility features, here are some important things to keep in mind:

- Don't set the Description on Labels: The screen reader will automatically read the text of a label.

- Avoid setting Description on Entry or Editor elements on Android: This can interfere with TalkBack actions. Instead, use the Placeholder or Hint property to provide accessible information.

- On iOS: If you set the Description property on a control that has child elements, it may prevent the screen reader from accessing the child elements. This can lead to incomplete information being presented to users relying on assistive technologies.

SettingsPage with SemanticProperties:

```
<Label Grid.Row="0" x:Name="PreferredFormulaLabel"
       FontSize="Large"
       TextColor="{StaticResource AccentColor}"
       SemanticProperties.Hint="Displays the currently selected
       formula"
       SemanticProperties.HeadingLevel="Level1" />

<Label x:Name="ChangeFormulaLabel" Grid.Row="1" Text="{Binding
Source={x:Static resources:Appres.ChangePreferredFormula}}"
       TextColor="{StaticResource PrimaryColor3}"
       SemanticProperties.Hint="Label for picker to change the
       formula"
       SemanticProperties.HeadingLevel="Level1"/>

<Picker Grid.Row="2" Title="{Binding Source={x:Static
resources:Appres.SelectFormula}}"
        x:Name="RepMaxFormulasPicker"
        TitleColor="{StaticResource PrimaryColor2}"
        BackgroundColor="{StaticResource BackgroundColor2}"
        SemanticProperties.Description="{Binding
        Source={x:Reference ChangeFormulaLabel}, Path=Text}"
        SemanticProperties.Hint="Picker to change the formula"
        SemanticProperties.HeadingLevel="Level1"
        SelectedIndexChanged="OnFormulasSelectedIndexChanged"/>
```

AppTheme: Dynamic Theme Switching in .NET MAUI

In modern apps, users expect the ability to toggle between different themes, such as light mode, dark mode, or even accessibility-friendly themes. .NET MAUI has enhanced its support for dynamic theme switching, enabling us to build applications that adapt visually based on the user's preferences.

Adding Themes to the SettingsPage

To enable dynamic theme switching in your .NET MAUI app, you can follow these steps:

1. Define the resources for each theme in a ResourceDictionary. You need a code-behind for the resource. CSS won't work with themes:

```xml
<?xml version="1.0" encoding="UTF-8" ?>
<ResourceDictionary xmlns="http://schemas.microsoft.com/dotnet/2021/maui"
                    xmlns:x="http://schemas.microsoft.com/winfx/2009/xaml"
                    x:Class="AppForFitnessCore.Resources.Themes.ProtanopiaStyle">
    <Color x:Key="LabelTextColor">#006400</Color>
    <!-- Dark Green -->
    <Color x:Key="LabelBackgroundColor">#FFB6C1</Color>
    <!-- Light Pink -->
</ResourceDictionary>
```

2. Set a default theme in the app's App.xaml file:

```
<Application.Resources>
    <ResourceDictionary>
        <ResourceDictionary.MergedDictionaries>
            <ResourceDictionary Source="Resources/
            Themes/DefaultStyle.xaml" />
```

3. Use DynamicResource markup extension for
    the styles:

```
<Label x:Name="SetColorTheme" Grid.Row="3" Text="Select
vision defiency theme."
        TextColor="{DynamicResource LabelTextColor}"
        FontSize="Large"
        BackgroundColor="{DynamicResource
        LabelBackgroundColor}"
        SemanticProperties.Hint="Label for picker to
        change colors for congenital color vision
        deficiencies."
        SemanticProperties.HeadingLevel="Level1"/>

<Picker x:Name="ColorThemePicker" Grid.Row="4"
Title="Color theme"
        TitleColor="{DynamicResource LabelTextColor}"
        BackgroundColor="{DynamicResource
        LabelBackgroundColor}"
        SemanticProperties.Description="{Binding
        Source={x:Reference SetColorTheme}, Path=Text}"
        SemanticProperties.Hint="Picker to change the
        color theme"
        SemanticProperties.HeadingLevel="Level1"
        SelectedIndexChanged="OnThemeChanged"/>
```

4. Load theme when user changes theme by removing
    and adding:

```
private void OnThemeChanged(object? sender,
EventArgs e)
{
    if (sender is not Picker picker) return;
    var selectedTheme = picker.SelectedItem?.
    ToString();

    if (string.IsNullOrEmpty(selectedTheme)
        || Application.Current is not App { Resources.
        MergedDictionaries: { } mergedDictionaries
        }) return;

    mergedDictionaries.Clear();
    switch (selectedTheme)
    {
        case "Protanopia":
            mergedDictionaries.Add(new
            ProtanopiaStyle());
            break;
        case "Tritanopia":
            mergedDictionaries.Add(new
            TritanopiaStyle());
            break;
        case "None":
            mergedDictionaries.Add(new DefaultStyle());
            break;
```

```
default:
    mergedDictionaries.Add(new DefaultStyle());
    break;
}
```

In earlier versions of the app, we used the StaticResource markup extension because the app didn't need to change themes dynamically at runtime. However, when we want to enable theme switching, we need to use DynamicResource instead. The DynamicResource markup extension allows resources to be updated at runtime, which is essential if we anticipate changing themes while the app is running.

The key difference is that DynamicResource maintains an active link to resource dictionary keys. When the resource values are replaced (e.g., when switching from light to dark mode), the changes are applied automatically to the UI elements that reference those resources (as shown in Figure 9-2). This enables seamless theme switching without restarting the app or manually refreshing the UI.

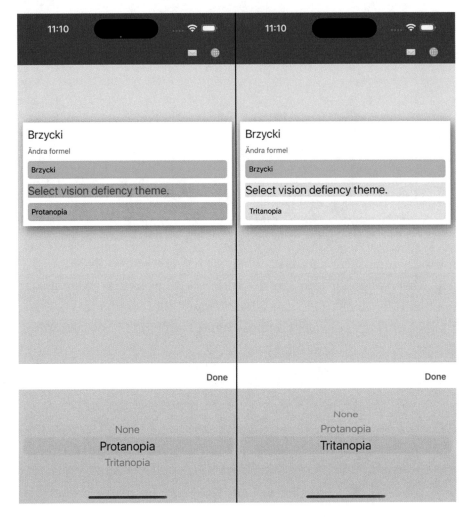

Figure 9-2. *Adding themes, for example, for visual deficiencies, is straightforward*

.NET MAUI also supports automatic theme switching based on the system's light or dark mode with AppThemeBinding, allowing us to adjust UI elements according to the system's theme settings. I've added a small example to the SettingsPage, which consists of XAML only and no extra code-behind. It really is that easy.

```
<Label Grid.Row="5"
       Text="{AppThemeBinding Light='Current system theme is
       Light', Dark='Current system theme is Dark'}"
       TextColor="{AppThemeBinding Light=Black, Dark=White}"
       FontSize="Large"/>
```

While this is a brief introduction, the possibilities for theming in .NET MAUI are extensive, and the official documentation provides many more examples.

Testing

AppForFitness currently doesn't have any tests, but we're about to change that. I'll walk you through the process of creating tests, with a particular focus on unit testing. When integrated into your development workflow, unit tests have a significant impact on improving code quality. They also serve as both design documentation and functional specifications, clearly defining how your app should behave.

Writing unit tests for platform-specific code is not common or practical for all solutions, because unit tests are meant to isolate and test logic, not platform-specific behaviors like UI rendering or OS-specific APIs (e.g., camera, GPS, or file system interactions). Platform-specific code is often tied directly to hardware or OS features, which makes unit testing less meaningful since those features typically need to be tested in their respective environments which can be done with UI tests, explorative testing, and other types of tests.

Unit tests are designed to test business logic in isolation without dependencies on the environment. For platform-specific code (such as checking DeviceInfo.Platform in .NET MAUI), the focus should be on abstracting this code into interfaces or services, which you can mock in tests.

Unit Tests

Instead of directly testing platform-specific code, a more common approach is to mock the platform-dependent behavior. This allows you to test how your app reacts to platform-specific scenarios (e.g., testing what happens when the app is running on iOS or Android), rather than testing the platform itself. Let's implement some unit tests:

1. Add new test project, for example, an xUnit test project. If you try to add a reference to the .NET MAUI project, you might get a message that it's not compatible (Figure 9-3).

Figure 9-3. *You might need to add conditions to your tags in the csproj file when adding a reference to a .NET MAUI project*

2. Update the .NET MAUI project to target .NET 8 as well, and add a condition to OutputType to only create an executable for the mobile apps:

```
<PropertyGroup>
    <TargetFrameworks>net8.0-android;net8.0-ios;
    net8.0</TargetFrameworks>
    <OutputType Condition="'$(TargetFramework)'
    != 'net8.0'">Exe</OutputType>
```

3. Make sure the class you are testing has abstracted dependencies that need to be mocked. For example, testing our SecureStorageService requires us to use the abstractions for Preferences, SecureStorage, and DeviceInfo, as well as creating a wrapper for Debugger.Attached. An easy way to create interfaces for existing classes is by (this is Rider specific, but many IDEs have this feature) right-clicking ➤ Refactor ➤ Extract Interface (Figure 9-4).

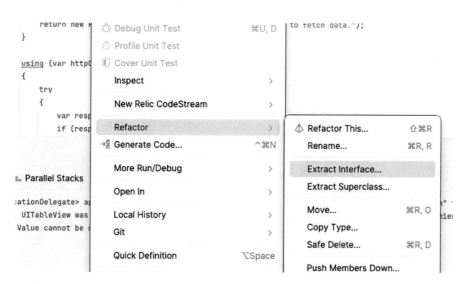

Figure 9-4. *Extract Interface is a nice feature that can help us quickly add a layer of abstraction*

Here is the refactored SecureStorageService.cs:

```csharp
public class SecureStorageService(
    IDeviceInfo deviceInfo,
    IDebugger debugger,
    IPreferences preferences,
    ISecureStorage secureStorage) : ISecureStorageService
{
    public async Task StoreDataAsync(string key, string value)
    {
        try
        {
            if (deviceInfo.Platform == DevicePlatform.iOS &&
            debugger.IsAttached)
            {
                preferences.Set(key, value);
            }
            else
            {
                await secureStorage.SetAsync(key, value);
            }
        }
        catch (Exception ex)
        {
            Console.WriteLine(ex.ToString());
            throw new SecureStorageException($"Failed to save
            data for key: {key}", ex);
        }
    }
}
```

Debugger wrapper:

```
public interface IDebugger
{
    public bool IsAttached { get; }
}
public class DebuggerWrapper : IDebugger
{
    public bool IsAttached => Debugger.IsAttached;
}
```

Dependency registrations:

```
builder.Services.AddSingleton(DeviceInfo.Current);
builder.Services.AddSingleton<IDebugger, DebuggerWrapper>();
builder.Services.AddSingleton(SecureStorage.Default);
builder.Services.AddSingleton(Preferences.Default);
builder.Services.AddTransient<ISecureStorageService,
SecureStorageService>();
```

4. Write tests:

```
public class SecureStorageServiceTests
{
    private readonly Mock<IDeviceInfo> _mockDeviceInfo = new();
    private readonly Mock<IDebugger> _mockDebugger = new();
    private readonly Mock<ISecureStorage> _mockSecureStorage
    = new();
    private readonly Mock<IPreferences> _mockPreferences
    = new();

    private SecureStorageService CreateService() =>
        new(
            _mockDeviceInfo.Object,
            _mockDebugger.Object,
```

```
        _mockPreferences.Object,
        _mockSecureStorage.Object);

    private DevicePlatform GetDevicePlatform(string platform)
    {
        return platform switch
        {
            nameof(DevicePlatform.iOS) => DevicePlatform.iOS,
            nameof(DevicePlatform.Android) => DevicePlatform.
            Android,
            _ => throw new ArgumentException($"Unsupported
            platform: {platform}")
        };
    }

    [Theory]
    [InlineData(nameof(DevicePlatform.iOS), true)]
    [InlineData(nameof(DevicePlatform.iOS), false)]
    [InlineData(nameof(DevicePlatform.Android), true)]
    [InlineData(nameof(DevicePlatform.Android), false)]
    public async Task StoreDataAsync_ShouldUseCorrect
    Storage(string platformName, bool isDebuggerAttached)
    {
        // Arrange
        var platform = GetDevicePlatform(platformName);
        _mockDeviceInfo.Setup(d => d.Platform).
        Returns(platform);
        _mockDebugger.Setup(d => d.IsAttached).
        Returns(isDebuggerAttached);
        var service = CreateService();

        // Act
        await service.StoreDataAsync("testKey", "testValue");
```

```
    // Assert
    if (platform == DevicePlatform.iOS &&
    isDebuggerAttached)
    {
        _mockPreferences.Verify(p => p.Set("testKey",
        "testValue", null), Times.Once);
        _mockSecureStorage.Verify(s =>
        s.SetAsync("testKey", "testValue"), Times.Never);
    }
    else
    {
        _mockSecureStorage.Verify(s =>
        s.SetAsync("testKey", "testValue"), Times.Once);
        _mockPreferences.Verify(p => p.Set(It.
        IsAny<string>(), It.IsAny<string>(),
        It.IsAny<string>()), Times.Never);
    }
}
// Code omitted
```

Integration Tests

Integration tests are designed to test how different parts of your system work together. Unlike unit tests, which focus on isolated components, integration tests verify that multiple components (such as classes, services, or modules) collaborate correctly.

Integration tests for a .NET MAUI application are no different from other integration tests. Here is one of the integration tests for the FitnessApiService:

```csharp
public ApiServiceIntegrationTests()
{
    _client = new HttpClient();
    _client.BaseAddress = new Uri(Config.BaseUrl);
}

[Fact]
public async Task Get_Exercises_ReturnsSuccessAndCorrectData()
{
    // Arrange
    var endpoint = Config.ApiExercises;

    // Act
    var response = await _client.GetAsync(endpoint);
    response.EnsureSuccessStatusCode();

    var responseData = await response.Content.
    ReadAsStringAsync();

    // Assert
    Assert.NotNull(responseData);
    var exerciseCatalogue = JsonSerializer.Deserialize<Exercise
    Catalogue>(responseData);
    Assert.NotNull(exerciseCatalogue);
    Assert.NotEmpty(exerciseCatalogue.Exercises);
}
```

I had to make significant refactoring efforts to implement the integration tests, but this ultimately led to a more loosely coupled code structure, which is widely considered a good practice. The result is code that's now more testable, maintainable, and flexible for future changes. That said, it's important to note that this app remains a sample project designed to highlight specific features and challenges. The code is kept as concise and readable as possible to showcase concepts clearly. If you're interested in the details of these changes, you can find all the updates in the related commit.

UI Tests

UI testing in .NET MAUI is somewhat different from Xamarin.Forms, primarily due to changes in the underlying framework and tools used for UI testing. However, the fundamental concept remains the same: UI testing involves automating interactions with the user interface of your application to validate that the app behaves as expected. UI testing is beyond the scope of this book, but I do want to mention two tools (and I'm sure there are more that will pop up over the next few years):

- Appium: This is still a robust, widely used solution that fully supports .NET MAUI apps across Android and iOS, leveraging the WebDriver protocol to interact with mobile applications.

- Maestro: A fast-growing tool with an evolving feature set that could be an excellent fit for .NET MAUI testing on mobile platforms.

Exploratory Testing and Scenario-Based Testing

Exploratory testing and scenario-based testing will always be a golden standard and very important part of developing stable apps. Our test team for the app at Plejd is almost as big as the developer team, and they use a variety of automated UI tests, exploratory testing, scenario-based testing, alpha and beta testing, and more.

Even though we have unit and integration tests and UI tests, they always find edge cases that we've missed. Exploratory testing is a manual testing technique where testers actively explore the application without following a predefined set of test cases. The focus is on discovery, investigation, and learning as testers interact with the application in real time, finding issues that might not be uncovered through traditional scripted testing.

As the name implies, scenario-based testing is when tests are created based on specific cases or scenarios. It is also commonly referred to as use case testing. It's similar to regression testing which is the process of running a suite of tests, including previously defined scenarios, after changes are made to the application to ensure no new defects are introduced.

Performance

According to Google/SOASTA research, if a page takes one to three seconds or more to load, bounce rates increase by 32%. While I don't know how this would translate to a mobile app, I can imagine the user's impatience and expectations are very similar.

There's no denial that there is limited tooling for performance and memory profiling due to the complexity of building cross-platform applications, but there are some. While this performance profiling is out of scope for this book, I do want to discuss how we can improve performance. If you'd like to learn more about profiling .NET MAUI applications, have a read here: `https://github.com/dotnet/maui/wiki/Profiling-.NET-MAUI-Apps`.

Performance in .NET MAUI apps is crucial for providing a smooth user experience across different platforms. Microsoft recommends several strategies to optimize MAUI app performance:

- Optimize layout: Use efficient layouts like Grid and StackLayout, and avoid deeply nested structures. Review complex XAML files, like src/AppForFitnessCore/Views/ProgressPage.xaml to ensure optimal layout.

- Reduce binding overhead: Use compiled bindings where possible. For example, in your ProgressPage.xaml, you could use compiled bindings for frequently updated properties. Compiled bindings are enabled by default; you might have seen this on some of the pages:

```
[XamlCompilation(XamlCompilationOptions.Compile)]
public partial class ProgressPage
{
```

The line can be removed as its default, but you can set the option to Skip. That would also mean that errors will be reported at runtime instead of compile time. Skip is for obvious reasons not recommended.

While the code above was declared for the type, you can also set it for the assembly, forcing the option:

```
[assembly: XamlCompilation(XamlCompilationOptions.Compile)]
```

- Image optimization: Use appropriate image sizes and formats. Review the images in your Resources/Images folder to ensure they're optimized for mobile devices.

- Asynchronous programming: Use async/await for I/O-bound operations. In your FitnessApiService.cs, ensure all network calls are asynchronous.

- Virtualization: For long lists, use CollectionView with virtualization. If your app displays long lists of exercises or workout history, consider implementing this.

- On-demand loading: Load data and UI elements only when needed. In your ProgressPage.xaml.cs, consider implementing lazy loading for chart data.

- Reduce app startup time: Minimize initialization work in App.xaml.cs. Review your src/AppForFitnessCore/ App.xaml.cs to ensure only essential tasks are performed at startup.

- Use platform-specific optimizations: Leverage native APIs where possible for better performance. You could explore this in your platform-specific code in the Platforms folder.

- Profile and monitor.

- Optimize data access: If you're using a local database, ensure queries are optimized. Review any database operations in your services.

You can find additional recommendations and information here: `https://learn.microsoft.com/en-us/dotnet/maui/deployment/ performance`

Memory

Memory leaks are a performance nightmare and known to be difficult to profile and identify. While some performance tools can give a pretty good indication of where there's a problem, it's hard to say if it's due to memory without specifically monitoring memory usage. You can use tools for memory profiling or the good old-fashioned way of manually monitoring memory usage by the process (if you are running a simulator) or by using tools. For example, for iPhone apps on Mac, you could use Xcode memory debugger, Xcode Instruments, Activity Monitor, third-party profiling tools, or even iOS Settings storage for the app.

But I've also come across a fun little library you can add to the app, MemoryToolkit.Maui. MemoryToolkit.Maui is a NuGet package designed specifically for .NET MAUI applications to help developers detect and diagnose memory leaks, and I'm going to use it to demonstrate why memory leaks, in particular memory leaks, are difficult to identify even with the help of tools. Let's have a look:

1. Add the NuGet package AdamE. MemoryToolkit.Maui.

2. Add to builder:

```
if DEBUG
    // Configure logging
    builder.Logging.AddDebug();

    // Ensure UseLeakDetection is called after logging
        has been configured!
    builder.UseLeakDetection(collectionTarget =>
    {
        // This callback will run any time a leak is
            detected.
        Application.Current?.MainPage?.DisplayAlert
        ("☠Leak Detected☠",
            $"🧟{collectionTarget.Name} is a
            zombie!", "OK");
    });
#endif
```

3. Add to page:

```
<ContentPage xmlns="http://schemas.microsoft.com/
dotnet/2021/maui"
                xmlns:x="http://schemas.microsoft.com/
                winfx/2009/xaml"
                xmlns:mtk="clr-namespace:MemoryToolkit.
                Maui;assembly=MemoryToolkit.Maui"
                x:Class="ShellSample.MainPage"
                mtk:LeakMonitorBehavior.Cascade="True">
    <!-- All child views are now monitored for
leaks. -->
</ContentPage>
```

Whenever it detects a potential memory leak, it will output to the console and display a pop-up. You can remove the pop-up message if it bothers you; simply remove the callback code.

Adding this to the pages in AppForFitness yielded a lot of memory leaks, all of them when navigating away from a page. And I suspect that the memory leak detection library is reporting false positives due to the way AppShell manages page instances. This is a common misunderstanding when working with memory profiling tools in the context of navigation frameworks like Shell.

Here's why this might be happening.

Shell's page caching: AppShell, by design, keeps page instances in memory for performance reasons. When you navigate between tabs or pages defined in the Shell, it doesn't typically dispose of these pages. Instead, it caches them for faster navigation in the future, which is nice and what we often (but not always) want.

Many memory leak detection tools, including the MemoryToolkit. Maui you're using, often work by tracking object allocations and checking if they're still in memory after certain operations (like navigation). If an object persists in memory when the tool expects it to be gone, it may flag this as a potential leak.

False positives: In the case of Shell, pages that are kept in memory intentionally might be flagged as leaks because they're not being garbage collected when the detection tool expects them to be.

Memory Leak in Action

To demonstrate a memory leak, I've added an extra page in the app with a memory leak, for educational purposes.

Let's break down the memory leak in this example:

- Event subscription without unsubscription: In the OnAppearing method, we're subscribing to the _triggerEventButton.Clicked event each time the page appears. However, we never unsubscribe from this event. This means that every time the page appears, we're adding a new event handler without removing the old ones.

- Closure over large object: Each event handler we create captures a reference to a large object (1MB byte array) in its closure. This means that as long as the event handler exists, this large object cannot be garbage collected.

- Strong references: The button (_triggerEventButton) holds strong references to all its event handlers. As we keep adding handlers without removing them, the button ends up holding references to multiple 1MB objects, one for each time the page appeared.

- Persistent memory allocation: Every time OnAppearing is called, we're effectively adding another 1MB to the memory that can't be freed. This memory remains allocated because

  - The button holds a reference to the event handler.

  - The event handler holds a reference to the large byte array through its closure.

- Garbage collection ineffectiveness: When we force garbage collection, it can't free these objects because there's still a chain of strong references leading to them: Button ➤ Event Handler ➤ Large Byte Array.

- Accumulation over time: In a real app, if this page is navigated to and from repeatedly, the memory usage would continue to grow, potentially leading to performance issues or even out-of-memory errors in extreme cases.

Keeping an eye on memory usage is a quick way to find possible memory leaks. If memory usage keeps increasing and you aren't doing anything that should increase memory usage, then you might have a leak.

Monitoring overall memory usage is a good first step in identifying potential memory leaks. If memory usage consistently increases without apparent reason, it's a red flag. The MemoryLeak Toolkit, like many similar tools, has both strengths and limitations.

It's primarily designed to detect leaks in UI elements and views, and it may not catch all types of leaks, especially those related to non-UI objects or complex scenarios.

It can produce false positives (indicating a leak where there isn't one) and false negatives (missing actual leaks). The WorkoutPage is a perfect example of a leak that might not be caught by the MemoryLeak Toolkit.

This is because the leak is occurring due to event handler subscriptions, which are not directly tied to the UI elements that the toolkit primarily monitors.

False negatives: In our case, the toolkit gave warnings for controls on other pages but missed the actual leak in the WorkoutPage. This highlights the importance of not relying solely on automated tools for leak detection.

To summarize, to identify and address memory leaks, it's best to use a combination of

- Automated tools like the MemoryLeak Toolkit

- Manual code review

- Profiling tools

- Careful testing and monitoring of memory usage patterns

It's crucial to understand what each tool can and cannot do. The MemoryLeak Toolkit is excellent for catching certain types of UI-related leaks, but it's not a comprehensive solution for all memory issues.

Trimming and AOT for Performance Optimization

Beyond the optimizations we discussed earlier, there is also AOT and trimming. Mobile platforms like iOS and Android have constrained memory and resources, so shaving a couple of megabytes makes a big difference. There are two key techniques we can add to our already optimized apps that we've only briefly mentioned so far, Ahead-of-Time compilation (AOT) and trimming. These two can improve startup times and responsiveness and reduce app size. Let's have a closer look, starting with trimming.

Trimming

Trimming is a .NET SDK feature that removes unused assemblies and code from your app, which helps reduce the final size of the app. When you build your app, in particular for release, there might be many parts of the libraries you use, such as the .NET Base Class library, that aren't used by the app. Trimming removes what isn't being used, keeping only the essential bits. By analyzing the code and determining what is used and what isn't used, the trimming tool is able to remove what isn't referenced by your code. We covered trimming incompatibilities earlier in the book, but as a refresher here they are:

- Reflection-based serializers (hence why we removed Newtonsoft).

- Runtime code generation via JIT (System.reflection. Emit usage)

- Dynamic assembly loading (the trimmer won't know what to use and what to trim away if you dynamically load assemblies)

- And some Windows-specific incompatibilities, such as

  - C++/CLI

  - COM marshaling

  - WPF and Windows Forms

Configuring Trimming

In your .csproj file, you can enable or adjust trimming by setting the PublishTrimmed property to true. Here's a basic example:

```
<PropertyGroup>
  <PublishTrimmed>true</PublishTrimmed>
</PropertyGroup>
```

You can also specify different trimming granularity using the TrimMode property, such as

- Full (default)

- Partial (only assemblies that have opted in to trimming)

Opting in assemblies when TrimMode is set to partial is done with the TrimmableAssembly tag:

```
<ItemGroup>
  <TrimmableAssembly Include="MyAssembly" />
</ItemGroup>
```

While trimming is powerful, it's important to test your app thoroughly after enabling it, as aggressive trimming can sometimes remove parts of the framework or libraries that your app needs at runtime.

For more information, refer to the official documentation on trimming: `https://learn.microsoft.com/en-us/dotnet/core/deploying/trimming/trimming-options`.

Ahead-of-Time (AOT) Compilation

Ahead-of-Time (AOT) compilation is another powerful optimization for .NET MAUI apps, particularly for iOS. In AOT compilation, the code is compiled directly into native machine code ahead of time, instead of relying on the Just-in-Time (JIT) compilation that occurs at runtime. This results in significant improvements to startup times and can lead to performance gains during the app's execution.

AOT is mandatory for iOS apps because Apple prohibits JIT compilation. This means all iOS apps built with .NET MAUI are fully AOT compiled into native ARM assembly code. However, AOT can also be used on Android to improve performance, though it is not mandatory.

Configuring AOT

To enable AOT compilation for your Android app, you can add the following configuration to your .csproj file:

```
<PropertyGroup>
  <RunAOTCompilation>true</RunAOTCompilation>
</PropertyGroup>
```

Additionally, you can enable LLVM optimization by adding UseLLVM. LLVM (Low-Level Virtual Machine) is a collection of modular and reusable compiler and toolchain technologies designed for developing compiler front ends and back ends that help further optimize AOT on Android.

```
<PropertyGroup>
  <RunAOTCompilation>true</RunAOTCompilation>
  <UseLLVM>true</UseLLVM>
</PropertyGroup>
```

However, AOT compilation does come with trade-offs. While it can greatly improve startup time and overall performance, it can also increase build times and, in rare cases, the size of the app. Therefore, test and test some more. It's important to configure and test these optimizations carefully to strike the right balance between app size and performance and functionality if your app relies on dynamic assembly loading or reflection-based serializers.

Summary

This chapter wrapped up the migration of the AppForFitness app and provided a comprehensive guide for transitioning a Xamarin.Forms app to .NET MAUI. For my team, who had to migrate a mature and complex application (unlike our example app here), the journey was challenging, especially under tight deadlines. Despite the difficulties, we are thrilled with the results. The migration introduced exciting improvements, including faster deployments to simulators and devices, more unified controls and views, and an opinionated use of design patterns that has guided us toward a more maintainable codebase. This is particularly rewarding given the previously fragmented nature of cross-platform development.

That said, the journey doesn't end here. As .NET MAUI continues to evolve, we have to stay informed about new updates, improvements, and best practices. Ongoing maintenance is key to ensuring our app remains robust, scalable, and ready to embrace the future of mobile development. Staying current is just as important as the initial migration itself, and our goal is to keep refining our app as .NET MAUI matures.

In the appendix, you'll find a detailed list of resources to help you stay up to date, along with a section on common migration problems and known issues. If anything is missing, don't hesitate to reach out to Apress or me. We're always here to help you on your .NET MAUI journey.

Resources and Further Reading

Staying informed and equipped with the right resources is crucial when navigating the evolving landscape of mobile development, especially when migrating from Xamarin.Forms to .NET MAUI. Whether you're tackling technical challenges, optimizing performance, or learning new features, having access to reliable documentation, tutorials, and tools is essential. In this appendix, I'll list some of my favorite and valuable resources, including official documentation, community blogs, podcasts, GitHub repositories, and virtual macOS solutions.

Microsoft Official Documentation

The Microsoft Official Documentation should be your primary source for information. It is exhaustive and kept up to date, and if you find inaccuracies, you can always do a pull request or submit an issue to the documentation repository.

> **Microsoft Official Docs—Migration Guide**
> This is the official guide from Microsoft that provides step-by-step instructions for migrating an app from Xamarin.Forms to .NET MAUI.
> ```
> https://learn.microsoft.com/en-us/dotnet/
> maui/migration/migrate-from-xamarin-forms
> ```

© Iris Classon 2025
I. Classon, *Migrating from Xamarin.Forms to .NET MAUI*,
https://doi.org/10.1007/979-8-8688-1215-6

.NET Upgrade Assistant

A tool provided by Microsoft to assist in migrating Xamarin.Forms projects to .NET MAUI.
`https://learn.microsoft.com/en-us/dotnet/core/porting/upgrade-assistant-overview`

Blogs and Articles

There's no lack of blogs and articles on .NET MAUI, but these are some of my favorites:

Gerald Versluis—Migrating to .NET MAUI

This blog post series by Gerald covers the essential steps and common issues encountered during migration, offering practical insights.
`https://blog.verslu.is/`

James Montemagno's Blog

A key contributor to Xamarin and .NET MAUI, James Montemagno provides valuable advice and tips on migrating. His YouTube videos are fantastic, and you'll find the link further down.
`https://montemagno.com/`

Dev.to Community Articles on MAUI

Various developers have shared their migration experiences, best practices, and challenges, making this a good place to discover real-world examples.
`https://dev.to/t/maui`

JetBrains Blog (Rider and ReSharper)

JetBrains is the company behind the Rider IDE and other tools that simplify our lives as developers. Their products, such as ReSharper and dotTrace, are widely used in the .NET community to enhance productivity, improve code quality, and optimize performance. JetBrains continuously invests in creating cutting-edge tools that cater to cross-platform development, and their blog is a great resource.

```
https://blog.jetbrains.com/dotnet/
```

Third-Party Vendors' Blogs (and UI Components)

A little fun fact: I used to work for Telerik as a technical evangelist. Telerik is a company that provides .NET component suites for frameworks like .NET MAUI (as well as other platforms). Third-party vendors, like Telerik, often maintain active blogs that cover both general .NET MAUI topics and tooling-specific content. These companies frequently employ technical evangelists whose job is to create educational content for developers. As a result, their blogs tend to be highly detailed and prolific, offering valuable insights into using their tools effectively within the .NET ecosystem.

Telerik/Progress Blog
Telerik is well known for its powerful UI controls and libraries, and they have been an important resource for Xamarin developers. As they transition to .NET MAUI, their blog is full of useful migration insights.
```
https://www.telerik.com/blogs
```

DevExpress Blog

DevExpress, like Telerik, is also a third-party vendor. Their blog, which is kept up to date by technical evangelists, covers step-by-step guides on profiling and performance optimization in .NET MAUI applications.
`https://community.devexpress.com/blogs`

Syncfusion Blog

Syncfusion is another vendor with great tools and an active blog.
`https://www.syncfusion.com/blogs/`

Videos and Tutorials

For many developers, learning through videos and hands-on tutorials is one of the most effective ways to grasp new concepts and technologies. I often watch these while I get my indoor runs in or while I'm waiting for the build pipeline to finish.

Microsoft Learn

Microsoft Learn is Microsoft's official learning platform, offering a wide range of content on various technical topics. The platform features code-along series, deep-dive tutorials, and quick singular videos that cover topics from basic introductions to advanced concepts. You can follow along with interactive tutorials at your own pace. For those working with .NET MAUI or other Microsoft technologies, you might even spot me in some of these videos.
`https://learn.microsoft.com/en-us/training/paths/build-apps-with-dotnet-maui/`

DotNetConf Sessions

Conference sessions, especially from .NET
Conf 2023 and 2024, where several speakers
demonstrated migrating to MAUI.
`https://dotnetconf.net/`

Pluralsight

Pluralsight is similar to Microsoft Learn with a
broad catalog of courses and video format learning
resources. Many of the courses have code samples
you can download.
`https://www.pluralsight.com/search?q=maui`

GitHub Repositories and Sample Code

I highly recommend subscribing to the .NET MAUI GitHub repository if
you do active .NET MAUI development. It's a great way to stay up to date!
In addition, don't hesitate to submit issues, join the discussions, or even
do a pull request.

.NET MAUI GitHub Repository

`https://github.com/dotnet/maui`

Sample Code Repository:
`https://github.com/dotnet/maui-samples`

.NET MAUI Community Toolkit

The .NET MAUI Community Toolkit repository
includes migration examples and community
contributions related to MAUI functionality.
`https://github.com/CommunityToolkit/Maui`

MemoryLeak Sample Repo

This repository demonstrates common memory leaks in Xamarin.Forms and .NET MAUI, helping developers identify and fix memory management issues during the migration process.
`https://github.com/rolfbjarne/memoryleak`

AI Tools

There are many AI tools available to developers, and new ones are emerging on a weekly basis. Tools like Rider AI Assistant and GitHub Copilot are incredibly useful, not only as pair programmers or sources of documentation (always ask for links and double-check information!) but also for nontraditional use cases. I've been using Copilot and Augment to help me understand the source code for .NET MAUI and third-party libraries that I use.

For instance, Augment can analyze a folder of code files or specific files and help you quickly extract insights. You can ask questions like

- How does the builder in MauiProgram work?

- Which types are marked as obsolete?

- How is a handler implemented? (For example, "Please show me how ButtonHandler is implemented.")

These tools can save significant time in code analysis and understanding, especially when navigating complex frameworks or third-party libraries.

Example Using Augment

Augmentlink

Certainly! I'll explain how ButtonHandler is implemented using the provided source code as an example. The ButtonHandler follows a common pattern used in .NET MAUI for implementing handlers across different platforms. Let's break it down.

Base Implementation

The base implementation of ButtonHandler is defined in ButtonHandler.cs:

```
public partial class ButtonHandler : IButtonHandler
{
    public static IPropertyMapper<IButton, IButtonHandler>
    Mapper = new
    PropertyMapper<IButton, IButtonHandler>(ViewHandler.
    ViewMapper)
    {
        [nameof(IButton.Background)] = MapBackground,
        [nameof(IButton.Padding)] = MapPadding,
        [nameof(IButtonStroke.StrokeThickness)] =
        MapStrokeThickness,
        [nameof(IButtonStroke.StrokeColor)] = MapStrokeColor,
        [nameof(IButtonStroke.CornerRadius)] = MapCornerRadius
    };
    public static CommandMapper<IButton, IButtonHandler>
    CommandMapper = new
    (ViewCommandMapper);
```

```
    public ButtonHandler() : base(Mapper, CommandMapper)
    {
    }
    // ... other members
}
```

This base class defines the property mapper and command mapper, which are used to map properties and commands from the cross-platform abstraction to platform-specific implementations.

Platform-Specific Implementations

The ButtonHandler is then implemented for each platform (Android, iOS, Windows, etc.) using partial classes. For example, in ButtonHandler. Android.cs:

```
public partial class ButtonHandler : ViewHandler<IButton,
MaterialButton>
{
    protected override MaterialButton CreatePlatformView()
    {
        MaterialButton platformButton = new
        MauiMaterialButton(Context)
        {
            IconGravity = MaterialButton.IconGravityTextStart,
            IconTintMode = Android.Graphics.PorterDuff.Mode.Add,
            IconTint = TransparentColorStateList,
            SoundEffectsEnabled = false
        };
        return platformButton;
    }
    // ... other platform-specific methods
}
```

Interface Implementation

The ButtonHandler implements the IButtonHandler interface, which is defined in IButtonHandler.cs:

```
public partial interface IButtonHandler : IViewHandler
{
    new IButton VirtualView { get; }
    new PlatformView PlatformView { get; }
    ImageSourcePartLoader ImageSourceLoader { get; }
}
```

The rest of the dialogue is omitted, but this shows how powerful AI tools can be for learning!

Forums and Discussion Platforms

There are plenty of social media and discussion platforms where .NET MAUI is a hot topic. However, it can be easy to get overwhelmed by the volume of discussions, and it's sometimes difficult to filter out useful information from the noise. Despite this, I've found Reddit and Stack Overflow to be especially valuable. These platforms offer active communities that regularly share insights, ask and answer technical questions, and discuss updates on .NET MAUI.

Reddit: .NET MAUI Community
The .NET MAUI subreddit is an active community where developers share migration strategies and solutions to common issues.
https://www.reddit.com/r/dotnetmaui/

Stack Overflow: .NET MAUI Tag
Stack Overflow is great for asking questions and troubleshooting migration challenges.
https://stackoverflow.com/questions/tagged/.net-maui

Renting a Virtual Mac for Development

For many developers working with .NET MAUI, especially those on Windows machines, having access to a macOS environment is critical. You may need a macOS machine for building, testing, and deploying iOS and macOS applications. Since acquiring and maintaining a physical Mac can be costly or impractical for some, renting a Virtual Mac (VM) is an excellent alternative. Here are some of the most popular services where you can rent virtual or remote Mac environments:

MacinCloud
MacinCloud is one of the most popular services for developers who need access to macOS environments. It offers various subscription plans, including Managed Servers, Dedicated Servers, and Pay-As-You-Go options.
https://www.macincloud.com/

MacStadium
MacStadium specializes in providing enterprise-grade Mac infrastructure, including Mac mini and Mac Pro hosting.
https://www.macstadium.com/

VirtualMacOSX

VirtualMacOSX provides macOS instances for iOS
app development, with pricing tiers based on usage.
`https://virtualmacosx.com/`

Summary

Staying up to date is vital in the fast-paced world of software development.
Migrating an app from Xamarin.Forms to .NET MAUI is just the start of
the journey. Once your app is up and running in .NET MAUI, ongoing
maintenance is essential to ensure it remains performant, secure, and
compliant with the latest platform changes. This is where continuous
learning becomes crucial. By subscribing to official documentation,
reading blogs, listening to podcasts, and following relevant discussions,
you'll be better equipped to manage your app long after the initial
migration.

APPENDIX B

Common Errors and Problems

Software development often feels like a delicate balance between creating something functional and unraveling the inevitable complexities that arise along the way. Debugging, fixing, and resolving issues is an integral part of every developer's journey, and migrating to .NET MAUI from Xamarin. Forms is no exception.

Appendix B covers some of the common environment errors and problems encountered during the migration process.

Environment Errors and Problems

When migrating to .NET MAUI, several common errors may occur during the build process. Below are some of the most frequently encountered issues and their solutions.

Error: NETSDK1178

Error Message:

```
Error NETSDK1178 : The project depends on the following
workload packs that do not exist in any of the workloads
available in this installation: Microsoft.NETCore.App.Runtime.
```

© Iris Classon 2025
I. Classon, *Migrating from Xamarin.Forms to .NET MAUI*,
https://doi.org/10.1007/979-8-8688-1215-6

```
AOT.Cross.net8.ios-arm64 Microsoft.NETCore.App.Runtime.AOT.
Cross.net8.iossimulator-arm64 Microsoft.NETCore.App.Runtime.
AOT.Cross.net8.iossimulator-x64
```

Solution:

Add a global.json to the project and specify the correct .NET version, ensuring you're not using a prerelease version.

Error: ILLINK: MT2301 and NETSDK1144

Error Message:

```
ILLINK: Error MT2301: The linker step 'Setup' failed during
processing.
Microsoft.NET.ILLink.targets(87,5): Error NETSDK1144:
Optimizing assemblies for size failed.
```

Solution:

Adjust the MtouchLink and PublishTrimmed properties in your project's .csproj file:

```
<PropertyGroup>
    <MtouchLink>SDKOnly</MtouchLink>
    <PublishTrimmed>false</PublishTrimmed>
</PropertyGroup>
```

Incompatible Java or Android SDK

Error Message:

```
"Java SDK path not found" or "Android SDK not recognized."
```

Solution:

Ensure that the correct Java SDK version is installed and that your Android SDK path is correctly configured. Setting the AndroidSdkDirectory in your project's .csproj file often resolves the issue.

Xcode or macOS Dependencies

Error Message:

"Xcode path not found" or "Xcode version incompatible."

Solution:
Ensure you have the correct version of Xcode installed from the App Store, and check that the Xcode path is set correctly in your IDE (Visual Studio or Rider). If the latest Xcode version is not supported, downgrading can help.

XAML and Namespace Errors

Errors related to namespaces and missing components are common in the migration process. One particularly frequent error involves InitializeComponent.

CS0103 'InitializeComponent' Does Not Exist

Error Message:

XAML pages not being included or Error CS0103: The name 'InitializeComponent' does not exist in the current context

Solutions:

- Namespace mismatch: Ensure the x:Class attribute in the XAML file matches the namespace in the code-behind.

- Build action: Set the build action of the XAML file to MauiXaml.

- Restart Visual Studio: Sometimes, a simple restart fixes the issue.

- Remove special characters: Ensure the project path does not include special characters like #.

- Update dependencies: Check that Microsoft.Maui. Controls is properly referenced.

Platform-Specific Errors

When dealing with platform-specific builds, errors relating to platform configuration and deployment might arise.

MinimumOSVersion Value Mismatch

Error Message:

The MinimumOSVersion value in the Info.plist (11) does not match the SupportedOSPlatformVersion value (11.0) in the project file.

Solution:
If the version is defined in the .csproj file, remove the entry from the Info. plist file:

```
<SupportedOSPlatformVersion Condition="$([MSBuild]::GetTarget
PlatformIdentifier('$(TargetFramework)')) == 'ios'">11.0
</SupportedOSPlatformVersion>
```

Virtual Device Issues for Android

Error Message:

"Android emulator not found" or "Android device deployment fails."

Solution:

Ensure that you have an Android Virtual Device (AVD) configured properly using the AVD Manager in Android Studio. Check if the correct API level is installed for the target emulator.

Simulator Not Found or Runtime Version Mismatch

Error Message:

"Failed to locate any simulator runtime matching options."

Solution:

This occurs when the necessary simulator (e.g., iOS 17.5) isn't installed in Xcode.Open Xcode on your Mac, go to Settings ➤ Platforms, and ensure the required iOS simulator version is installed. You can also run xcrun simctl list devices to list available simulators.

IDE-Specific Errors

IDE errors can occur when configurations or paths are incorrect, especially when using third-party IDEs like Rider.

Platform Folders Not Found (Rider)

Error Message:

Namespace does not correspond to file location, must be: 'AppForFitnessCore.Effects'

Solution:

Select the correct namespace provider in Rider or ensure the namespaces are correctly mapped.

NU1101 Unable to Find Package Microsoft.Maui. Controls

Issue:
This error occurs when a project cannot find a required NuGet package.

Solution:
Ensure that your NuGet package sources are correctly set up in Visual Studio. If necessary, update the package using the NuGet Package Manager or by running the dotnet restore command.

iOS-Specific Errors

iOS deployment and linking often cause challenges during the migration process.

Application Bundle Not Generated

Error Message:

```
Application bundle wasn't generated after deployment
```

Solution:
Ensure that you have selected the iPhoneSimulator as the deployment target in Visual Studio.

Android-Specific Errors

Android-specific issues often arise around intents, deep linking, and memory handling.

Error: Deep Link Doesn't Work

Problem:

OnAppLinkRequestReceived not called.

Solution:

Override the OnNewIntent method in MainActivity to route deep link requests:

```
protected override void OnNewIntent(Intent? intent)
{
    base.OnNewIntent(intent);
    var dataString = intent?.DataString;
    if (intent?.Action == Intent.ActionView && !string.
    IsNullOrEmpty(dataString))
    {
        Microsoft.Maui.Controls.Application.Current?.SendOnApp
        LinkRequestReceived(new Uri(dataString));
    }
}
```

Android Emulator Won't Start

Issue:

The emulator hangs or freezes during startup, often taking 10–30 minutes and then crashing.

Solution:

Check emulator storage and memory allocation.

App Crashes After Launch

Issue:

After upgrading to .NET 8, some developers report that their app crashes immediately on the Android simulator, especially when using certain authentication libraries like MSAL. MSAL (Microsoft Authentication Library) is a library that enables authentication and token management for Microsoft identity platforms.

Solution:

This could be related to compatibility with the Android 34 emulator or new .NET 8 features. Switching back to Android API 33 may resolve the issue for now. Ensure all libraries are up to date.

UI Issues

Migrating UI components can lead to missing elements or incorrect layouts.

Shell.ToolbarItems Not Showing on iOS

Description:

ToolbarItems may not appear correctly due to a known bug in iOS.

Solutions:

- Add ToolbarItems to each page individually.

- Use a TitleView instead:

```
<Shell.TitleView>
    <VerticalStackLayout HorizontalOptions="End">
        <Button Text="✉" Clicked="OnEmailClicked" />
```

```
        <Button Text="🌐" Clicked="OnLanguageSettingsClicked" />
    </VerticalStackLayout>
</Shell.TitleView>
```

Test Project Errors

Errors in test projects can stem from missing targets or misconfigured frameworks.

Assets File Target Missing

Error Message:

```
Assets file doesn't have a target for 'net8.0-android/
android-arm64'.
```

Solution:

Check your .csproj to ensure the appropriate target platforms are included:

```
<TargetFrameworks>net8.0-android;net8.0-ios;net8.0</
TargetFrameworks>
```

Submitting Issues

Even with thorough preparation, some errors will inevitably require external help. If you encounter bugs or issues, consider submitting them to the official .NET MAUI GitHub repository:

```
https://github.com/dotnet/maui/issues/new?assignees=&labels=t%2
Fbug&projects=&template=bug-report.yml
```

Index

A, B

Accessibility
    automation properties, 171
    considerations, 172
    features, 171
    SemanticProperties, 171
    SettingsPage, 173
Ahead-of-Time (AOT), 197, 198
Android project, 134, 135
AOT, *see* Ahead-of-
    Time (AOT)
AppForFitness
    code structure, 33
    migration process, 34
    MVVM pattern, 33
    navigation, 139
    1RM (*see* One Rep Max (1RM)
        progress)
    side-by-side migration
        compatibility package, 92
        dependencies, 89–91
        long-term support (LTS), 86
        namespaces, 91–94
        output window, 87
        OxyPlot, 89, 90
        SDK version, 88

AppShell navigation, 138, 139
Artificial Intelligence (AI)
    Augmentlink, 207
    ButtonHandler, 207
    code/specific files, 206
    Copilot/Augment, 206
    interface implementation, 209
    Mac environments, 210
    platform-specific
        implementations, 208
    social media/discussion
        platforms, 209

C

CLI, *see* Command-line
    tool (CLI)
Command-line tool (CLI), 82, 83
    VS (*see* Visual Studio)

D

Deep link navigation, 144
Dummy implementation, 111
Dynamic theme switching
    (AppTheme), 174–179

© Iris Classon 2025
I. Classon, *Migrating from Xamarin.Forms to .NET MAUI*,
https://doi.org/10.1007/979-8-8688-1215-6